ASSESSING ENGLISH LANGUAGE LEARNERS

The Author

Lorraine Valdez-Pierce is an Associate Professor in the Graduate School of Education at George Mason University, a position she has held since 1992. She designs and teaches courses for teachers of English language learners on assessment, literacy development, standards-based curriculum design, and education policy. For the past decade, as part of a long-term school-university partnership in northern Virginia, she has led teachers in developing performance-based assessments of oral language, reading, and writing. A consultant to several state education agencies, as well as the U.S. Department of Education, she is the author or editor of over 55 books, articles, and monographs. She is also co-author with J. M. O'Malley of a pioneering book, *Authentic Assessment for English Language Learners: Practical Approaches for Teachers.* She holds a Ph.D. in Linguistics from Georgetown University and, in 1982, was the recipient of a Fulbright Grant for study in Italy.

Student Assessment Series

ASSESSING ENGLISH LANGUAGE LEARNERS

Lorraine Valdez-Pierce

Glen W. Cutlip
Series Editor

nea
NATIONAL EDUCATION ASSOCIATION
www.nea.org
Great Public Schools for Every Child

Library of Congress Cataloguing-in-Publication data.

Pierce, Lorraine Valdez, 1952-
    Assessing English language learners / Lorraine Valdez-Pierce.
        p. cm. — (Student assessment series)
    Includes bibliographical references.
    ISBN 0-8106-2076-6
        1. Educational language—Study and teaching—Foreign speakers.
    2. Education, Bilingual—Ability testing. 3. Education evaluation.
    I. Title. II. Series.

PE1128.A2P516 2003
428'.0071—dc21   2003046422

CONTENTS

Introduction vii

I.   English Language Learners 1

II.   Second Language Acquisition 5

III.   Standardized Tests 18

IV.   Performance-Based Assessments 37

V.   Scoring Tools 58

VI.   Professional Development 71

Appendices 81

References 92

INTRODUCTION

The field of student assessment—from methodology and techniques to the use of results—is changing, and the changes offer opportunities and challenges for the work of educators.

Changes in student assessment have created new concerns for teachers, especially in the use of assessment results. Today, those results are being used for more than comparing an individual student's performance against a state or national norm, and for more than providing data for making program improvement decisions. They are being used to determine the success or failure of teachers and schools. Policy makers and others are using large-scale assessments to decide whether teachers and schools are providing an adequate education to all students and attaching consequences, positive and negative, on the basis of student assessment results. Amid these challenges, however, advances in student assessment practices supported by research are presenting educators with tools and strategies which can be integrated into classroom instruction to improve the learning of all students.

Nearly one-third of a classroom teacher's time is spent assessing and evaluating student performance. Indeed, many influential groups (National Board for Professional Teaching Standards, Interstate New Teacher Assessment Consortium, National Council for Accreditation of Teacher Education, and the Assessment Training Institute) have identified competence in student assessment as essential for the training and licensing of new teachers and upgrading the skills of practicing teachers. These groups estimate that less than one-half of the currently practicing teachers have received adequate training in student assessment, and yet their performance may be judged on their ability to match their student's performance to assessment criteria.

To help members and other educators keep abreast of the ever-changing field of student assessment, the National Education Association (NEA) has commissioned leading assessment and evaluation experts to write about these related issues from their own perspectives. Expert Dr. Valdez-Pierce, the author of this book on assessing English language learners, believes that traditional student assessment practices provide limited useful information on English language learners. She recommends assessment practices which are classroom-based and embedded in instruction as particularly effective for these students.

The NEA has developed the Student Assessment Series to help teachers—preschool through graduate studies—and other education employees improve their knowledge and skills in student assessment and achievement and hopes readers will find the series a valuable resource for current and future student assessment practices.

Glen W. Cutlip
Series Editor

In order to emphasize the English language acquisition process that learners experience, rather than stress their perceived deficiencies, the term "English language learners"(or ELLs) is used throughout this book in place of "limited English proficient" (or LEP), the more conventional term used by the U.S. Department of Education and some states.

English Language Learners

As another school day ends and she prepares materials to take home, Marge Smith wonders what she can do to assist her three non-native speakers of English. These students are in the English as a second language (ESL) program, where they get special help for one hour each day. Yet, they are not making fast enough progress to keep up with the rest of her seventh-grade earth science class. They also require individual attention, and they are not at all ready to perform well on the state-wide standardized tests.

As a secondary school science teacher, Marge has not been prepared to deal with these students, and she feels at a loss to help them. Why couldn't they have been put in her class after they had learned to speak and read English? And what can she do now to help them learn? Wouldn't it be unfair to the rest of her class to treat these students differently? Shouldn't they be held to the same standards as everybody else? How can she determine the type of progress they are making?

Although Marge wants to help her English language learners, she just doesn't have enough energy left over at the end of the day to find the time or information she needs to help them. Her school system has not provided grade-level teachers with much useful information on how to teach these students. Because of this, she has resorted to seating them in the back of the room with worksheets until she can find something better for them to do. At least this way they are not taking time away from preparing the rest of the class to take the statewide standardized tests.

Schools have been undergoing tremendous demographic changes over the past two decades. As the number of culturally and linguistically diverse students attending public schools in the United States continues to rise each year, there is a greater than ever likelihood that each and every teacher and school will one day be faced with the responsibility of educating these children. While the majority of public school teachers speak only English, over one-fifth of children in U.S. public schools come from homes where a language other than English is spoken, and the number of children in public schools who are not yet proficient in the English language is growing at more than twice the number of native speakers of English (Kindler 2002). More than two-thirds of these students are enrolled in elementary schools, and over half of them will most likely be enrolled in middle and secondary schools over the next decade. Most of them come from economically disadvantaged homes. Spanish is the native language of the majority—about three-fourths—of school-age English language learners. Two-thirds of these students are concentrated in a few large states: California, Texas, New York, Florida, and Illinois (August and Hakuta 1998; Heubert and Hauser 1999; Kindler 2002).

Purpose

The purpose of this book is to familiarize teachers having little or no background in teaching English language learners (ELLs) with effective approaches for assessing these students. Accurate assessment practices and policies are critical for ensuring that ELLs get access to instructional programs that meet their learning needs. Inappropriate assessment approaches can lead to inaccurate identification of English language learning needs, improper program placement, insufficient monitoring of student progress, and long-term failure of school programs (Cummins 1984). On the other hand, appropriate assessment approaches have the potential to accurately identify language and content learning needs and help prepare students for grade-level classrooms and standardized tests. While the focus of this book is on assessment, any discussion of promising approaches to student evaluation must begin with an overview of the language learning process and of what works in instruction to promote learning for ESL learners. This book aims to answer questions similar to those Mrs. Smith faced in the opening vignette and to provide information on other topics relevant to the assessment of English language learners.

Two Types of Assessment

Teachers of English language learning students will most likely be faced with questions about two types of assessment that differ in purpose and administration—standardized tests and classroom-based assessments. Both types are discussed in this book, and suggestions are provided to help teachers conduct each equitably and effectively with ELLs. Standardized tests are those administered by most state education agencies annually for the purpose of educational accountability. These assessments are summative or based on end-of-year learning, are administered according to standardized procedures and timetables specified by the state, and are required to demonstrate acceptable psychometric and technical properties, such as validity and reliability. The scores on these types of tests, which include items that are typically in multiple-choice format, are interpreted using norm-referenced and/or criterion-referenced scales, and consequences are often attached to the scores.

Classroom-based assessments, on the other hand, are those formative and informal assessments that teachers conduct with students on a daily basis. These assessments are as varied as the teachers who use them. Classroom-based assessments usually reflect content area objectives and instructional activities that each teacher has conducted with students. Innovative classroom approaches to assessment can be embedded in the instructional activities themselves, as in the case of teacher observations, peer and self-assessments, and student performances and demonstrations. The primary purposes of classroom-based assessment include monitoring student learning, redirecting instruction, and providing feedback to the learner.

Summary

In order to make appropriate decisions about assessing English language learners, we need to first understand the second language learning process. In Chapter II, teachers are provided with a brief overview of the second language acquisition process in order to set realistic expectations for the performance and language proficiency attainment of children who have not yet become proficient in the English language.

Chapter III addresses the reality of statewide testing programs and identifies promising policies and practices used in the assessment of English language learners. The chapter examines the limitations of traditional forms of assessment, including teacher-made tests, for the purposes of evaluating the achievement of ELLs.

Chapter IV describes the power of alternative, innovative approaches to assessment for ELLs.

Chapter V provides teachers with examples of effective, research-based approaches and activities that can be used for scoring the assessments of ELLs.

Finally, Chapter VI discusses the need for long-term professional development on assessment for all teachers working with ELLs and includes recommended steps for getting started with practical assessments of ELLs.

For those seeking further information on this topic, the Appendices provide resources ranging from books and research articles to videotapes and Internet web sites.

II.

Second Language Acquisition

In response to rapidly changing demographics and the increasing numbers of culturally and linguistically diverse learners in the public schools, new and different means of instruction and assessment must be used to help these students meet state and local standards for learning. Many teachers have begun to re-evaluate their approaches to instruction and assessment in response to the research on second language acquisition.

The nature of language proficiency and the time it takes to learn a language, including stages in language development, individual and classroom variables that impact the rate and levels of language learning, and implications for realistic expectations for language learning and academic achievement are discussed, and appropriate assessment approaches recommended.

Two Misconceptions about Language Learning

Teachers often make assumptions about students that shape their expectations for each student's performance. It is imperative, therefore, to address misconceptions about children who are in the process of learning English in school settings. Two major misconceptions about language learning are based on confusion between surface or conversational aspects of language and cognitive aspects of proficiency more closely related to the academic language needed for school (Cummins 1994b). The first misconception deals with educators making inferences about the intelligence or logical thinking of English language learners based on their familiarity with or command of standard English. The second misconception is related to the first, in that students' fluency in oral English leads to mistaken assumptions that all aspects of English proficiency—including reading and writing—have also been mastered.

To address these misconceptions, it is necessary to clarify the relationship between language proficiency and the academic achievement of English language learners. Cummins (1994b) has proposed the most useful research-based framework to date for understanding this relationship. He proposes making a fundamental distinction between conversational and academic English. These two types of language can be differentiated along two continuums: the degree of language context provided in the communicative setting and the level of cognitive demand made on the language learner (see Figure 2-1).

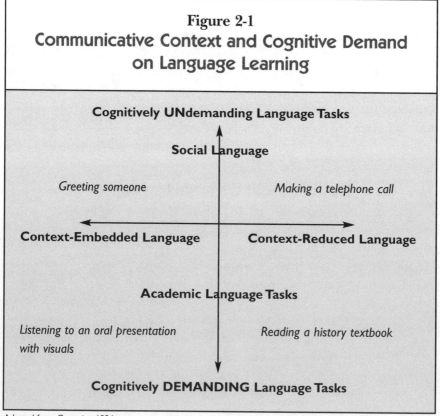

Figure 2-1
Communicative Context and Cognitive Demand on Language Learning

Cognitively UNdemanding Language Tasks

Social Language

Greeting someone   *Making a telephone call*

Context-Embedded Language   **Context-Reduced Language**

Academic Language Tasks

Listening to an oral presentation   *Reading a history textbook*
with visuals

Cognitively DEMANDING Language Tasks

Adapted from Cummins, 1994a

For example, teachers may be perplexed by the English language learner who appears to be fluent when speaking yet is not learning to read or is doing poorly in school subjects. How can this be when the student seems to be able to communicate orally in English? This puzzling case reflects the stark difference between conversational or social language and academic language. ELLs who have high levels of social language proficiency will not necessarily have the same levels of proficiency in academic language.

For students learning English, the communicative setting can range from contextualized or context-embedded language to situations that are relatively decontextualized and provide few context clues to meaning. For purposes of learning, language tasks run the gamut from those that make few cognitive demands to those that place an overwhelming cognitive demand on language learners, especially those with limited prior schooling or who lack literacy skills in the native language.

Conversational language of daily social interaction (greeting, requesting, describing) is typically acquired in settings rich in context that can help bring meaning to the language. For example, children at play may refer to toys and manipulatives as they act out a situation. Young adults learning how to drive a car must perform physical tasks when following directions for operating a vehicle. When tangible items, physical actions, and visible cues such as facial expressions and gestures are used to enhance meaning, the language can be said to be contextualized. Contextualized language or context-embedded communication allows participants to actively negotiate meaning through face-to-face interaction, situational cues, and concrete objects. **Context-embedded language** is typical of language used in social settings outside the classroom.

Academic language, on the other hand, is typically decontextualized or context-reduced and relies less on physical cues and more on linguistic cues for meaning, so that full comprehension of the message relies on a high level of English language proficiency. **Context-reduced language** used in classroom settings occurs without the tangible, physical, and visible cues to meaning that are available in face-to-face communication or in purposeful exchanges involving gestures, real artifacts, and visuals. Textbooks with tiny print, little white space, and few illustrations or visuals to assist comprehension contain clear examples of context-reduced language. Most beginning and intermediate level ELLs will find content area textbooks, especially in the social studies and sciences, particularly difficult. Language learners faced with the task of extracting meaning from print-dense texts will be significantly more challenged than when faced with context-embedded social language tasks.

While both context-embedded and context-reduced learning activities can be found in schools, only context-embedded situations can facilitate language acquisition. Where context is missing, teachers will need to provide it by activating prior knowledge and bringing interactive, hands-on, collaborative experiences to learning. Putting a student in the back of the classroom with a worksheet (as Marge does in the opening chapter) will not help him or her acquire the language. It would be better to include this child in the instructional activity by pairing him or her with a supportive buddy who can help make sense of the activity through face-to-face, hands-on interaction.

Communicative tasks place certain cognitive demands on language learners. In social, context-embedded settings, cognitive demands will be relatively low. In the classroom, however, learning tasks are generally cognitively demanding. The most cognitively demanding tasks are those that introduce new concepts, processes, and vocabulary to the language learner. Cognitively demanding learning tasks that require memorization, categorization, generalization, and inference for discovering rules of the language and internalizing these rules for learning are minimally supported by contextual or interpersonal cues. This is what makes language difficult for ELLs in school.

Implications for Instruction and Assessment

It is easy to confuse English language ability or lack thereof—as measured by traditional assessments—with intelligence or learning disabilities, and educators need to be careful not to make program placements, especially those to special education, contingent upon oral language alone or on the disparity between social and academic language. Educators need to avoid erroneously assuming that IQ tests and other tests normed on native speakers of English show the academic potential of English language learners when what they actually show is their current level of functioning in academic English.

To assist language learners in comprehending assessment tasks, teachers need to modify instruction to provide contexts for interactive negotiation of meaning. They can do this by incorporating any of the following strategies in their assessment tasks:

- activating prior knowledge on the topic to motivate interest and build self-confidence in accomplishing the assessment task;

- using concrete, tangible items, visuals, and graphics to bring meaning to assessment tasks;

- designing assessment tasks that provide opportunities for working with a partner or a team, including hands-on learning, and allowing for non-verbal (for beginners) and simplified verbal responses; and

- teaching and assessing learners' use of learning strategies that can help them succeed on assessments of reading by cutting through extraneous information in texts, such as reading comprehension questions before reading the text.

The primary goal of this type of assessment is to find out what students can do with what they know and how well they respond to instruction, rather than to determine only how well they can function in English.

Stages of Language Development

Learning English as a second, third, or fourth language is for bilinguals and multilinguals a process similar to learning the native language. The learner goes through several distinct stages, makes errors as he or she goes, acquires the oral language through personal interaction, and needs direct instruction to learn how to read and write. At all stages, syntactical and grammatical errors will occur as a natural part of the language learning process. The more difference there is between the student's native language writing system and English, the more challenging it will be to learn to read and write in English. Error correction has not been shown to have a positive effect on language acquisition, but error correction that focuses on meaning appears to be more helpful than that which emphasizes form or grammar. Learners will correct their own errors once they internalize more accurate forms of language use, and error correction will not expedite the language learning process (Ellis 1994).

Implications for Assessment

Implications for assessment include the need to:

- focus on fluency and accuracy and not be overly concerned about every grammar or pronunciation error that students make; correcting errors in oral language or writing will not accelerate the language learning process, and

• understand that fluent speakers of English may not yet be ready to show what they know through well-constructed, error-free writing in English.

How Long Does it Take to Learn Another Language for School?

Research on English language learning suggests that while social language can be acquired in one to two years, academic language or the type of language needed to attain grade-level norms on standardized tests in English may take between five and ten years to develop (Collier 1992; Cummins 1994b; Ramirez, Yuen, Ramey, and Billings 1991). As discussed in the previous section, it takes a long time to develop academic language for school because tasks are more cognitively demanding than conversational tasks, and unlike social language, academic language is context-reduced. In addition, students in the general population are not waiting around for the ELL students to catch up with them on standardized tests. ELL students are essentially following a moving target, because native speakers of English are typically increasing literacy and content area skills with each year of instruction (Thomas and Collier 2002; Cummins 1994b).

Implications for Instruction and Assessment

The research on how long it takes to learn a second language for school has serious implications for assessment, because decisions about ELLs are often made on assumptions about how long it takes to learn a language. We can draw the following implications from second language acquisition research for assessment of ESL students:

• First, fluency in speaking skills does not necessarily mean that students are ready to take standardized tests.

• Second, language learners need time for processing and thinking in their new language, and assessments that allow for flexible time limits can go a long way toward relieving test anxiety and promoting self-confidence.

• Third, proper assessment procedures have to be in place so that English language learners are not inappropriately placed in special education programs due to a lack of achievement as measured by standardized tests. Assessments of intelligence and academic achievement are likely to underestimate the academic potential of these students.

- Finally, teachers must have realistic expectations for student performance on standardized tests. ELLs will take longer to reach standards-based learning goals and grade-level norms on standardized tests than native speakers of English.

We could suggest to Marge Smith in the opening vignette that she be patient with her English language learners and provide them with personally meaningful, interactive opportunities for learning and that she document student growth using classroom-based assessment tools that are sensitive to individual progress, such as anecdotal records, teacher observation checklists, and scoring rubrics.

Individual and Classroom Variables in Language Learning

While English language learners go through similar stages of language acquisition, not all students will learn the language at the same rate or to the same degree. In this section, we look at individual and classroom factors that influence the rate of attainment and ultimate level of language proficiency that ELLs will achieve. First, it is important to understand that language learning is the result of complex interactions between individual learner variables and what the teacher can provide in the classroom setting (see Figure 2-2). A supportive whole-school context is also essential for promoting the academic achievement of culturally and linguistically diverse students. Second, we need to recognize that the presence of any combination of these variables will differ from one learner to another, resulting in great variation among language learners.

Comprehensible input. Research on the language learning process suggests that the learner's ability to make personal meaning out of instructional contexts facilitates learning. Language and content that motivate the learner and promote comprehension can provide comprehensible input, which is necessary for learning to occur (Krashen 1994). Teachers can use specific instructional approaches to help language learners comprehend content area materials presented in the classroom.

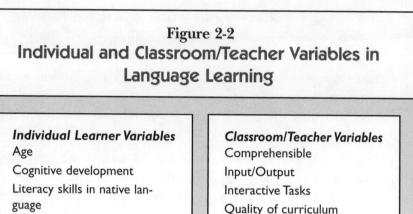

Figure 2-2
Individual and Classroom/Teacher Variables in Language Learning

Individual Learner Variables
Age
Cognitive development
Literacy skills in native language
Personality
Self-confidence, motivation

Classroom/Teacher Variables
Comprehensible Input/Output
Interactive Tasks
Quality of curriculum

Language Proficiency
Academic Achievement

Adapted from Cummins, 1994b.

Communicative interaction can help provide comprehensible input. Students need to have opportunities to negotiate meaning with other ELLs and with native speakers of English in both oral and written English. Encouraging active use of oral and written language that promotes language learning has been called comprehensible output (Cummins 1994b). ELL students need opportunities to interact with others through both oral and written language and to receive feedback on that language.

Individual learner variables affecting quantity and quality of input and output include having an outgoing personality and self-confidence in one's identity and ability to learn. Personality variables, however, appear to be more related to interactional style in conversation, while cognitive variables are more related to the development of academic language.

It is not enough to talk at students, expose them to the English language all day, or focus on teaching grammar and spelling. Students must be assisted in making sense of incoming messages. Teachers need to meet learners half-way by focusing on meaning. There are a number of ways to accomplish this, and many regular education teachers are already doing some of these things, including:

- Finding out what students already know on a topic and relating new information to that prior knowledge.

- Learning about and appealing to students' interests.

- Presenting an engaging curriculum.

- Integrating all four language skills (reinforcing oral presentations or lectures with gestures, dramatizations, manipulatives or real objects, think-pair-share activities, notes, graphic organizers, video, large print on easy-to-read overhead transparencies, or other visual aids).

- Paraphrasing, presenting key points through different media.

- Modeling and demonstrating strategies and processes.

- Teaching students how to maximize their language development by teaching learning strategies such as summarizing, analyzing, and synthesizing.

- Providing for collaborative pair and group work on problem-solving tasks.

- Promoting physical engagement and interaction.

- Including support for native language use wherever possible.

Assessment activities need to include as many of the above listed approaches as possible in order to reduce the amount and difficulty level of language being presented to students. The goal, after all, is to provide students with access to the curriculum, not to lock them out of it.

Affective Considerations. In order for ELLs to do their best in a classroom setting, they need to feel accepted and free to take risks. They also need to feel that their language and culture are not inferior to that of native speakers of English. When students are anxious about not being able to communicate in their native language or make friends in school, about having to pass standardized tests, and about competing with native speakers of English in content areas, they will not be able to concentrate on learning. The teacher has a responsibility to establish a supportive classroom environment that accepts and welcomes culturally and linguistically diverse language minority students.

Instruction and assessment tasks should be sensitive to students' native language and culture. Asking a student not to use his or her native language in the classroom conveys a negative message to the student about the value of his or her cultural identity. Students need to think in the native language as they transition to English; indeed, it is impossible for them not to.

Age. Contrary to popular belief, younger children do not necessarily acquire a new language faster or better than older learners. The only aspect of language learning where younger children would appear to have an advantage over older learners is in acquiring native-like pronunciation. Students who begin learning a new language in secondary school may not be able to lose their native language "accent" completely. Because they are more cognitively mature, however, older learners may have an advantage over younger learners in the efficiency with which they learn English, especially if they bring prior knowledge and educational experiences (including literacy in the native language) that can help them tackle cognitively difficult tasks. Otherwise, ELLs who lack reading and writing skills in their native language will face the triple challenge of learning both oral and written language while also acquiring content area concepts. Without individual help or personalized attention to meet their literacy needs, students who lack literacy in the native language may never acquire high levels of literacy skills in English. This may be the kind of student Marge Smith is facing in the opening vignette. These students will need tutoring in reading and writing in order to get to a functioning level of literacy in English.

Implications for Instruction and Assessment

To get an idea of what it would be like to be in the shoes of a language learning student in school, a native speaker of English need only imagine moving to a country such as Japan or Russia where he or she does not know the language. Both of those countries have totally different writing systems from that of English, so the English speaker would need to acquire not only oral language for social communication and learn the cultural rules for school routines and for activities outside of school. At the same time, one would also need reading and writing skills as well as learning strategies to extract information from content area textbooks in history, biology, or algebra written in the unknown language.

Teachers need to provide a comfortable, supportive, anxiety-free environment in order to encourage a language learner's best performance on tests or other types of assessment. Assessments that provide comprehensible input through opportunities for interaction (as in peer interviews, peer feedback, team projects, tackling real-world tasks, and getting the gist of an oral or written communication), that measure comprehensible output, and that allow for alternative ways to demonstrate knowledge—for example, through interviews, demonstrations, presentations of portfolios, and artistic renderings—can provide information that might not otherwise be available. In addition, it is essential to teach students how to monitor their own progress and to help them gain self-confidence in their own ability to learn. Finally, teachers need to include parents in the assessment process by sharing with them, through a translator or community liaison, if necessary, how they assess their students and what their expectations are for student performance. In this way, parents can be assisted in becoming allies in the learning process.

Summary

The purpose of this chapter is to help teachers develop an accurate picture of the language learning process so that they can use this information to set high but realistic goals for their English language learners. It also provides information for how to use specific approaches and strategies in instruction and assessment that can help enhance students' comprehension and consequent ability to perform assigned tasks.

When designing and using assessments for ELLs, teachers can:

• Activate prior knowledge.

• Use instructional strategies for assessment, including providing comprehensible input, opportunities for comprehensible output, and a supportive environment.

• Use assessments that provide comprehensible input and promote comprehensible output by modeling, demonstrating, using concrete objects and visuals, and activating prior knowledge.

- Use whole texts for assessment rather than discrete, isolated skills. Whole texts provide the context needed for comprehension.

- Integrate language with content instruction. Learning content material cannot be postponed until after students are perfectly fluent in English—it takes too long, and federal law requires states and local school systems to provide students with instruction that promotes both language development and academic achievement.

- Collaborate with ESL teachers to plan supportive instructional and assessment activities (e.g., peer tutoring, peer feedback, cooperative learning, process writing, team projects, and oral presentations) and continue to document student learning even after exit from the ESOL program. All content teachers need to recognize that for English language learners, they are also teachers of language.

- Integrate ELLs into the mainstream, providing opportunities for them to interact with native speakers.

- Design assessments that affirm students' cultural and linguistic identities, validate previous experiences, and promote self-confidence in their ability to learn, and encourage development of native language skills for the cognitive support they can provide.

- Conduct interviews with students periodically to determine how they monitor their own progress, their attitudes toward learning, and individual progress.

- Conduct ongoing observations of language development in listening, speaking, reading, and writing.

- Use teacher observation checklists to provide students with feedback on their language and content performance.

- Become an informed advocate for English language learners. Inform others about the need for flexible time limits on standardized tests and considerations for avoiding making incorrect assumptions about intelligence based on IQ tests and other standardized tests.

- Document what students can do with language and content; and keep anecdotal records of student growth in language and the content areas. Focus on fluency and accuracy rather than correcting errors.

- Involve parents, guardians, and older siblings in the assessment process so that the whole family can help the student meet learning goals.

- Be prepared to make a long-term commitment to supporting the academic achievement of English language learners.

III.

Standardized Tests

This chapter examines the reality of statewide standardized tests and their uses with and limitations for English language learners. It begins by looking at recent federal legislation that mandates state testing of all students and considers implications for including ELLs in statewide testing programs. It also examines the effects of excluding ELLs from these programs. Limitations of standardized tests used with ELLs are discussed in terms of validity, reliability, and test format. Types of assessments used in statewide testing programs are described and their appropriateness for use with ELLs discussed. Finally, implications for classroom-based assessment are presented, with suggestions for what teachers can do to help ELLs succeed on standardized tests.

Political Context: Federal Legislation

In January 2002, the reauthorized Elementary and Secondary Education Act (ESEA) was signed into law. The Act focuses on improving the educational achievement of all students, particularly economically disadvantaged and minority children, including those with limited English proficiency (or English language learners, as they are called in this book) and students with disabilities.

As a direct result of ESEA, schools are now responsible for testing all students at least once in grades 3 through 5, 6 through 9, and 10 through 12 in reading or language arts and mathematics. By academic year 2005-6, schools will be held accountable for, at a minimum, annual testing of all children in grades 3 through 8 in the same subjects. Any state receiving federal funds for Title I (Improving the Academic Achievement of the Disadvantaged) or Title

III (Language Instruction for Limited English Proficient and Immigrant Students) programs must comply with the requirements in both Title I and non-Title I schools.

States are specifically directed to report test scores for English language learners. They are also encouraged to test these students on "coherent and rigorous content...[and] advanced skills" (U.S. Congress 2001). The new law gives states and school districts flexibility in determining how they will help students meet state standards and how they will measure their academic progress. In addition, the state's tests must be statistically valid and reliable (Paige 2002).

ESEA represents the latest round of federal legislation promoting the use of standardized tests and large-scale testing for school improvement purposes. It also reflects increasing pressure to include larger numbers of students, including English language learners, in large-scale assessment programs. Schools need to show that ELLs are making *adequate yearly progress*, as defined by each state and to include high school graduation rates. Schools failing to make improvement will be identified by each state for a series of increasingly severe actions leading to improved achievement test scores. These actions include receiving additional assistance, implementing school choice, replacing school staff, reopening an under-performing school as a charter school, or allowing for its takeover by the state. Beginning test data has been collected by the states in academic year 2001-02, and states have 12 years in which to help all students achieve 100 percent proficiency in reading or language arts and mathematics (Paige 2002; U.S. Department of Education 2002).

To be included in standardized testing for ESEA, English language learners are to be provided with "reasonable accommodations...including to the extent practicable, assessments in the language and form most likely to yield accurate data on what such students know and can do in academic content areas, until such students have achieved English language proficiency." States are also encouraged to develop assessments in other languages for these students. In addition, alternative assessments may be developed to measure student progress. "Multiple, up-to-date measures of student achievement, including measures that assess higher-order thinking skills" are to be developed and used. English language learners are also to be assessed annually to measure their progress in listening, speaking, reading, and writing skills in

English. Test data are to be used specifically to improve their educational attainment (U.S. Congress 2001).

At least 95 percent of public school students are to be included in state education accountability systems, with no exclusion of ELLs from reading or language arts and math subtests. Adequate yearly progress will be based on the achievement of each subgroup, as well as on overall student achievement. States must set separate, measurable, annual objectives for ELLs, and this has led to a number of states beginning to set standards for this group of students.

Concerns for ELL Educators

ESEA, while laudable in its equity goals, is nevertheless problematic. Several concerns arise about the Act. Educational researchers suggest that policymakers' expectations exceed the ability of schools to make the sort of progress needed. One major concern is that the law requires steady increases in achievement from year to year, and this may not be possible due to measurement and sampling error. Most states have made annual increases of about one percent, far below the five to six percent required to make the 100 percent student proficiency rate by 2014 (assuming 30 percent of students are already at the proficient level in 2002).

Another concern is that the varying level of difficulty among state tests and passing scores will impact the number of students reaching the proficient level to be attained by all students by 2014. States are at different starting points and will have different distances to go to meet the law's requirements. The challenge of having all students meet high standards will be compounded with the inclusion of ELLs, who will actually have to outperform general education students in order to close the achievement gap in each school (Collier and Thomas 1998). (See also Chapter II on how long it takes to learn a language for school.)

Researchers predict that a substantial number of schools will be incorrectly identified as needing improvement as a result of the volatility of school-level scores. Moreover, the recommended consequences (such as providing school choice, reopening as a charter school, or allowing a state takeover) for schools that fail to meet improvement goals have little research base to support their effectiveness in improving schools.

ELL educators are also concerned about the assumption that the state tests are sensitive to growth resulting from classroom instruction. Assessment researchers caution that this may not be the case, leading to inaccurate inferences based on test results (Baker, Linn, and Herman 2002). Inaccurate inferences are made when

- there is a mismatch between the test and the classroom curriculum (highly likely in statewide standardized testing because broad-based measures are less likely to reflect instruction than classroom-based measures);

- the test is measuring background characteristics rather than what has been taught in the classroom;

- the test is insensitive to measuring change resulting from instruction; or

- scores may be inflated due to narrowing the curriculum and teaching to the test.

Each of these concerns is particularly important when interpreting test results for language minority students and ELLs. Inaccurate inferences mean test scores are not valid for the population being assessed. Assessment researchers recommend that states conduct studies to investigate these influences and to examine whether teachers are actually "advantaged by the information" provided by test scores for redirecting instruction and improving student learning (Baker, Linn, and Herman 2002).

State Assessments with Local Consequences for Students

While ESEA aims to improve the achievement levels of ELLs and other disadvantaged students and proposes consequences for schools failing to meet improvement goals for these students, it does not recommend consequences for individual students. Many states and local school systems do, however, propose serious consequences for students not making cut scores on standardized tests. For example, almost half the states require that students pass a standardized test in order to graduate from high school (Boser 2001). Most states use traditional, standardized, multiple-choice tests in the content areas for measuring student learning. Up to now, few states have taken into account the special learning and assessment needs of ELLs. Therefore, current assessment systems will pose a major challenge to states and school districts across the nation with regard to this population.

Mandating that ELLs pass a single state test or series of tests in order to graduate from high school, not considering other assessment information (such as SATs or ACTs, grades, and portfolios), presents a number of problems. One problem is that a single measure on one type of test cannot accurately reflect student learning or ensure that students have mastered all the standards set for high school (Heubert and Hauser 1999). A series of studies found that standardized tests in one state have already undermined educational quality and promoted discrimination against minority students by watering down the curriculum (McNeil 2000).

Another problem with requiring English language learners to attain a minimum score on a standardized test is that every standardized test administered in English in U.S. public schools is ultimately a test of the English language. Low scores for ELLs on standardized tests in the content areas will most likely not have the same causes as low test scores for native or proficient speakers of English. If students are not proficient in the language, they won't do well on the test, not necessarily because they don't know the subject matter of the test, but because they do not know enough English to read the test or follow oral or written directions and do not possess the vocabulary and content knowledge in English to be able to answer easy to intermediate level questions (Collier and Thomas 1998). If students do not have sufficient English language proficiency to show what they know on these types of tests, their resulting scores will lack validity and will not be reliable measures of what they know. Test results will underestimate a student's full extent of knowledge in a content area if he or she does not have the English language skills to read the directions or express his or her knowledge. English language learners need to first demonstrate the literacy skills needed to understand the items on the standardized tests before being required to take these tests.

In addition, high-stakes decisions such as graduation from high school need to be made with *multiple* measures rather than on the basis of a single test score (Collier and Thomas 1998; Heubert and Hauser 1999). Multiple measures ensure reliability of the information, similar to looking at snapshots of a person from different angles over a period of time. Multiple measures provide a fuller picture of a student's academic strengths and weaknesses than any single measure can show.

State Exemptions and Accommodations

Over the past decade, many ELLs have been excluded from the potential benefits of being counted in statewide testing programs (O'Malley and Pierce 1994). In 1998, almost all the states (46) allowed exemptions for ELLs from one or more statewide testing components for a specified number of years (Olson, Jones, and Bond 2001). Most of these exemptions used time in the U.S. or time in an ELL program as the criterion for exemption. A more useful criterion for exempting these students, however, is literacy at grade level in English as measured by valid and reliable measures (Heubert and Hauser 1999). ELLs will now become a focus of attention for inclusion in statewide education accountability programs. In order for this to happen successfully, however, several local processes must be in place:

(1) School systems need to use appropriate, valid, and reliable assessment procedures for identification and placement of students in ESL or bilingual education programs.

(2) Test scores for ELLs in reading, writing, and all content areas should be counted as part of school averages.

(3) Test scores for ELLs should not be used to prevent them from participating in extracurricular activities, since these are prime opportunities for developing oral language and interpersonal communication skills as well as for providing motivation for staying in school.

(4) ELLs should be held to the same high standards as other students and provided with opportunities to learn the same or similar subject matter on the tests.

(5) When ELLs are excluded from statewide tests required for the general student population (e.g., writing, social studies, science), alternate assessments should be made available to monitor the progress of this group.

States can assure the participation of ELLs in statewide testing programs by providing a range of accommodations for those who need them, as allowed by the law. The most commonly used accommodations include: providing longer and more flexible time limits (including extended sessions over multiple days), providing more breaks, and allowing the use of dictionaries or word lists (Fisher, Lapp, Flood, and Suarez 2001; Gottlieb 1999; O'Malley and Pierce 1994; Olson, Jones, and Bond 2001). Other accommodations include conducting testing in small groups, testing in a separate room, simplification or translation of directions; audiotaped instructions or directions; audiotaped responses; additional testing sessions; use of word processors; and reading the test to the student in English or the native language (if it is not a test of reading). A number of research efforts are underway to determine the effects of accommodations on ELLs, and although the findings are not yet definitive, it is clear that using a wide range of accommodations can increase the number of ELLs participating in statewide tests (Heubert and Hauser 1999).

Inclusion of ELL students in statewide accountability programs is essential to holding schools and state education agencies accountable for the progress of these students. To exclude them from statewide testing without requiring them to take alternate assessments of learning has serious ramifications for both the individual students involved and their schools. Accurate school and district-level data can only be attained when the test scores of all students, including ELLs, are counted. Statewide testing programs that inappropriately exclude ELLs' test scores will produce an inflated impression of the effects of state and local reforms and run counter to the tenets of fairness and equity that underlie the establishment of state standards (O'Malley and Pierce 1994).

Alternate Assessments

Alternate assessments and the use of multiple measures can provide more appropriate ways to include ELLs meaningfully in state testing. Three states—Illinois, Delaware, and Wisconsin—provide useful examples of alternate assessments used with ELLs at the statewide level (Gottlieb 1999).

In Illinois, one of the few states with the largest concentrations of English language learners, those exempted from the regular state test may take a standards-based English language proficiency test of reading and writing and a modified test of mathematics. The state is currently developing performance standards for the literacy test. Illinois also provides local school districts with guidance in developing thematic, content-area assessments for ELLs who are exempted from the state tests, with criteria specified in scoring rubrics.

Delaware has taken a two-pronged approach to alternate assessment of ELLs. First, it has developed, through the Portfolio Assessment of Limited English Proficient Students (PALS) Project, a set of menus for classroom-based assessment of language functions, including student work samples and examples of activities, tasks, and projects to be used on an ongoing basis. In addition, the state has designed secure performance activities and tasks that are administered at benchmark grade levels following the same time frame as the state testing program. Both classroom-based and state assessments are anchored by a uniform set of standards-based rubrics in English language arts.

Wisconsin recently developed one of the most innovative and promising statewide assessments so far for ELLs; this alternate assessment provides linguistic support through activities linked to classroom instruction and requires student responses that show what students know and can do in mathematics, social studies, science, and English language arts (Gottlieb 1999). Wisconsin has developed alternate academic content and performance standards for ELLs in grades 4, 8, and 10, that parallel those for the general student population. The Alternate Performance Indicators being piloted by the Wisconsin Department of Public Instruction for ELLs were developed by teachers and administrators throughout the state and are founded entirely on performance-based assessment at the classroom level. ELLs not participating in the Wisconsin Student Assessment System or the state test of Reading Comprehension must be assessed using the Alternate Performance Indicators. These alternate performance standards allow ELLs to become part of the state accountability system, increase the potential for ELLs to access general education programs, and form the basis for the development of alternate assessments to be used by classroom teachers (Gottlieb 1999).

Alternate assessments developed in Illinois, Delaware, and Wisconsin can serve as models for other states searching for ways to include ELLs in state education accountability programs. Alternate assessments are more appropriate for ELLs than norm-referenced tests (NRTs) and standardized tests because they provide reduced language demands through comprehensible input, context-embedded items, and a variety of response modes that more closely match classroom-based activities. Several psychometric challenges remain, however, in equating the scores from alternative assessments with the state standardized test for statewide reporting.

Parental Notification

In addition to providing accommodations and alternate assessments, school systems can facilitate participation of ELLs in statewide testing by notifying the parents about the purposes of and consequences associated with state testing. Until recently, most states have not had guidelines for notifying parents in their native language about the requirements and results of statewide testing (O'Malley and Pierce 1994). ESEA requires not only involving parents in the education process, but also notifying them of their children's test results as soon as possible after a state test is administered. Parental notification is especially important in the case of high-stakes testing, where students not passing the tests may be denied a high school diploma or suffer other consequences determined by local school district policy.

Limitations of Standardized Tests and other Traditional Forms of Assessment for English Language Learners

Many educators assessing the academic progress of culturally and linguistically diverse students are aware of the problematic issues raised by requiring these students to take multiple-choice and standardized tests. The use of traditional forms of testing persists today because the tests are objective, reliable, and cost-effective to administer and score. Although they may be reliable, however, they may not be valid for use with English language learners.

Validity

Standardized tests are not perfect, and they have limitations when used for making decisions about ELLs. The crux of the problem lies in using a standardized test with ELLs when they are not yet proficient in the language of the test. In such a case, test scores will not accurately reflect students' knowledge of the subject being assessed but will rather reflect their limited proficiency in English. Concerns regarding the shortcomings of standardized tests with ELLs stem primarily from issues related to validity and reliability. The more important the decision being made with test results (e.g., high school graduation, grade promotion, access to content courses), the more important it is to assure the validity and reliability of the tests.

The *validity* of an assessment measure or tool indicates the extent to which inferences based on test scores are appropriate for particular populations (Brualdi 2002). Validity is based on *how* a test is used, because tests are not inherently valid without regard to how the results are used (Heubert and

Hauser 1999). For example, a test claiming to be a test of history adminis-tered to ELLs who are at a beginning level of reading proficiency will not yield valid test scores of historical knowledge. Instead, it will indicate the stu-dents' lack of reading skills. Two types of validity—*content validity* and *conse-quential validity*—are particularly relevant for teachers working with English language learners.

Content validity refers to the match between the content of the assessment and that of the curriculum or classroom. When ELLs are assessed on the con-cepts and skills that they have been exposed to in the classroom, the assess-ment measure has content validity. *Consequential validity* refers to the way the assessment results are used to improve teaching and learning. When assess-ment results are used to redirect teaching and aid learning, the measure can be said to have consequential validity. When statewide testing programs do not supply teachers with useful information on how to support student learn-ing through instructional activities, these tests lack consequential validity.

Validity of an assessment can be reduced by the presence of systematic bias. Types of bias in standardized tests used with ELLs are: *cultural bias*, *assessment bias*, and *test* or *norming bias*. Teachers need to be aware of these threats to validity on statewide standardized tests because they limit the accu-racy of the inferences and subsequent decisions made for ELLs. These are described briefly below:

- *Cultural bias* refers to a test item that requires knowledge of a particu-lar culture's values and shared experiences while not intended for measuring this purpose. For example, if a test of reading requires knowledge of an American historical event, the test of reading becomes a history test. Standardized tests often include culturally-laden questions to assess reading skills and content area knowledge, but most ELLs may not be familiar with the cultural concepts present-ed and will respond incorrectly (Calkins, Montgomery, and Santman 1998; Hamayan and Damico 1991). In another example, given a ques-tion on a standardized test of reading in Japanese that requires cultur-al or historical knowledge, American students not having the prior knowledge required by the question will not be able to answer it cor-rectly, even when it is translated into English.

- *Assessment bias* occurs when assumptions made for the general popula-tion of test-takers are not valid for students whose culture is different from the majority culture. Cultural differences that can influence test scores include previous school setting or lack of schooling, previous life experiences in a significantly different environment, the value or non-value of competition in each student's culture, cultural mores, and the sociocultural status of the student's ethnic group within the larger society (Hamayan and Damico 1991). For example, most English language standardized tests assume the following elements are in place for students taking the test :

- grade-level appropriate English language proficiency, including shared cultural meanings between students and assessors;

- analytical thinking skills;

- acceptance of the value of competition with other students; and

- experience in taking timed, standardized tests (Garcia and Pearson, 1994; Hamayan and Damico 1991).

When these assumptions are not accurate for English language learners taking the tests, the scores will probably not be valid.

- *Test* or *norming bias* refers to the use of standardized tests that have not included sufficient numbers of language minority and ELLs as part of the norming group (Suzuki, Ponterotto, and Meller 2001). This means that if students from particular language minority groups have not been part of the norming data, the results of the standardized test are not valid (or accurate) for making inferences about these students (Garcia and Pearson 1994).

Although these types of bias probably cannot be totally removed from the testing process, their negative effects on the educational careers of ELLs can be limited. Teachers can recommend to local school systems and state departments of education that caution be used in making inferences about ELLs taking standardized tests designed for the general population of students. Policymakers, program administrators, and teachers need to take steps to reduce test bias on statewide tests by making the tests available for review by culturally and linguistically diverse educators involved in the preparation and licensing of teachers, ESL and bilingual education teachers, and parents and by using native culture and language informants for feedback on the tests.

Reliability

Reliability refers to the absence of random error in an assessment measure and the extent to which test scores result from student characteristics (Rudner and Schafer 2002). Random error can originate with items on the test itself, with variability of performance of the same student from one day to another, and from the way scores are determined. When random error is minimal, test scores will most likely be consistent from one administration to another. As with validity, the more important the decision resulting for the student based on the assessment results, the more essential it is for a high level of reliability to be established in the assessment measures and process. High levels of reliability can be established through the use of multiple measures, multiple raters, and clearly specified scoring criteria. For example, states typically use multiple raters to score student writing samples produced on statewide assessments of writing.

Types of Standardized Assessments

The type of test used to assess ELLs in statewide accountability programs can determine whether the test results will be valid and reliable. Three types of assessments used in standardized state assessment programs are ***norm-referenced, criterion-referenced, and performance-based assessments.*** These terms are not mutually exclusive, since a standardized assessment can be both norm-referenced and criterion-referenced. A brief description of the differences between the three types of assessments and their usefulness with ELLs is provided below and in Figure 3-1:

- *Norm-referenced tests (NRTs)* compare an individual English language learner's performance to the performance of students in the general population of test-takers in a national sample. NRTs are purposefully designed so that 50 percent of the students at each grade level score below average on each subtest. Examples of NRTs are the California Achievement Test, the Stanford 9, the Iowa Test of Basic Skills, and the Degrees of Reading Power Test. Scores are useful for determining where English language learners are in comparison with students in the general population of the same age and grade level taking the test. NRTs are not useful for monitoring growth in language development and conceptual understanding for ELLs who are new to the testing process or who are just beginning to acquire English language skills. These tests are especially inappropriate for ELLs during their first two to three years of instruction in English because of differences between their characteristics and those of the national comparison group (Collier and Thomas 1998). NRTs often lack content validity because they are not aligned with curricular activities. They are also not administered often enough to have consequential validity to be used to improve instruction for ELLs. The main reason why NRTs are not appropriate for monitoring the progress of ELLs is that these students do not yet have the English language skills needed to show what knowledge they really possess on a subject.

- *Criterion-referenced tests* (CRTs) compare student performance on content standards using a predetermined passing score for reporting. This passing score is often arbitrarily set through a political process informed by public opinion and field test data. Rather than compare ELLs with other students, CRTs determine each student's mastery of a subset of state or local standards. CRTs are useful for letting ELLs know what the learning targets are and for determining mastery of the standards once these students can read and write well enough to respond to the test items.

- *Performance-based assessments* (PBAs) ask students to apply knowledge in a practical or observable manner and are typically criterion-referenced in that criteria are used to judge student work. ELLs are asked to show what they know through demonstrations and by providing open-ended responses rather than answering questions about their knowledge. Most states require one type of PBA—writing samples—as part of statewide testing programs; these ask students to respond to an open-ended prompt. PBAs are appropriate for ELLs when they provide context-embedded, comprehensible input, flexible time limits, and a variety of response modes.

Multiple-Choice Format

Most norm-referenced and criterion-referenced standardized tests use primarily multiple-choice items for ease of administration and scoring, as well as their low cost, and because they are objective (only one right answer). Many books and articles have been written about the limitations of multiple-choice tests for assessing general education students, including:

- Measuring only a narrow range of lower order thinking skills.

Figure 3-1
Appropriateness of Statewide Assessments for English Language Learners

Type of Assessment	Useful For	Not Appropriate for
NRTs	• Comparing achievement of ELLs with that of national comparison group or other students in school system • Identifying relative areas of strength and weakness • Monitoring annual growth in basic skills in reading and content areas	• ELLs with less than 2-3 years of English language instruction • Making high-stakes decisions (e.g. high school graduation) • Making decisions for participation of ELLs in extracurricular activities • Monitoring growth of ELLs in ESL or bilingual education programs
CRTs	• Determining the extent to which ELLs (as a group or individuals) at each grade level have mastered state or local standards or curriculum objectives • Assessing basic skills • Monitoring growth of ELLs in ESL or bilingual education programs	• ELLs with less than 2-3 years of English language instruction • Making high-stakes decisions (e.g. high school graduation) • Making decisions for participation of ELLs in extracurricular activities
PBAs	• Monitoring ELLs' progress toward standards-based instructional objectives in the content areas • Making criteria clear to students • Assessing processes and products • Assessing complex, higher order thinking skills	• ELLs with less than 2-3 years of English language instruction • Making high-stakes decisions (e.g. high school graduation) • Making decisions for participation of ELLs in extracurricular activities

- Failing to measure application of critical thinking skills.

- Promoting a mismatch between classroom-based instruction and assessment, lacking content validity.

- Relying on memorization and recall of facts.

- Selecting what can be easily measured rather than what is important for students to be able to do in the real world.

- Overestimating what students know and can do.

- Trivializing teaching and learning and rewarding guessing.

- Promoting the false impression that every question has only one right answer (Herman, Aschbacher, and Winters 1992; Marzano and Kendall, 1998; Mitchell 1992).

In addition to the serious limitations of multiple-choice tests for native speakers of English, these tests pose problems for ELLs in the following ways:

- ELLs at a beginning level of English language proficiency or with limited exposure to English language tests (even with prior education in the native language) will most likely not be familiar with a multiple-choice format or with the other test-taking skills needed to do well on these tests.

- Multiple-choice formats have limited relevance to the meaningful, hands-on, collaborative learning that goes on in effective classrooms for English language learners.

- A lack of comprehensible input and context in multiple-choice tests contrasts with that provided through special instructional programs for ELL learners and is a significant limitation in helping these learners make sense out of a test-taking situation.

- If students have made progress in acquiring oral or written English skills—two areas of emphasis in English language programs—this progress will not be evident on multiple-choice tests.

Implications for Classroom-Based Assessment: What Teachers Can Do

Facing the prospect of preparing the English language learners in her class to take standardized tests in reading and mathematics six months from now,

Marge Smith is convinced that she needs help. Where should she start? Whom should she ask? What teaching approach is she already using that could be helpful to ELLs? What role can the grade-level teacher play in preparing ELLs to take and pass standardized tests? Should teachers teach to the test? Lucy Calkins and her colleagues have tried out a number of approaches with their own students and suggest that teachers develop a set of mini-lessons to teach students test-taking strategies. The strategies they suggest would work well for language minority students and ELLs who are at least at an intermediate level of reading in English (Calkins, Montgomery, and Santman 1998). Test-taking and other learning strategies suggested for mini-lessons include teaching students to:

- Enlarge reading texts on the overhead projector for think-aloud demonstrations, an activity that would work for ELLs because it would increase the likelihood of providing comprehensible input and lowering anxiety.

- Read the questions first, then read the passages to find the answers to the questions, as in a scavenger hunt; help students read test passages "with an awareness that the purpose for this reading...[is]...to answer the questions" (pre-reading strategies, reading with a purpose).

- Find out how many test questions they can hold in their minds as they search for answers in the reading passages (self-monitoring strategies).

- Focus on key vocabulary in each question to be better able to choose the best response (selective attention).

- Cover up some of the text with an index card to make it more manageable and less overwhelming (lowers anxiety and reduces cognitive load).

- Scan each page to check that each answer is filled in before turning to the next page (self-monitoring strategies.

- Check to see how many pages are in each section of the test in order to pace themselves (self-monitoring strategies).

- Check that they move between the test booklet and the answer sheet without missing an item (self-monitoring strategies).

Other ways teachers can assist ELLs in succeeding on standardized tests include:

- Facilitate language and concept development by teaching content area subjects for state or local standards-based objectives using teaching and assessment approaches that support language development (described in Chapter V) such as graphic organizers, visual aides, collaborative tasks, and writing key vocabulary and ideas presented in lectures or demonstrations on the overhead projector or chalkboard. An example would be using pair and small group activities when having students tackle cognitively demanding tasks in social studies and science. Teachers could also demonstrate how to use graphic organizers to brainstorm vocabulary and content area concepts.

- Promote learning in the content areas by devoting time in class each week to explicitly teaching and modeling learning strategies (such as reading and writing strategies) and higher order thinking skills (such as analysis, synthesis, and evaluation). For example, teachers can assist ELLs in reading with a purpose, locating main ideas in reading texts, orally summarizing the main ideas at the end of each paragraph, outlining supporting details, making inferences while reading, and re-reading passages to check for comprehension.

- Provide access to challenging and entertaining reading materials that students can take home and providing choices in what students read.

- Aim for a balanced approach to assessment, ranging from single-answer tests of basic skills to performance-based assessments that allow ELLs to demonstrate comprehension of key vocabulary and concepts. Teachers can use innovative, multiple and varied assessment tools to diagnose ELLs' needs in both English language and content. Federal legislation supports the use of innovative and alternative measures of learning for ELLs. Marge Smith could use her fill-in-the-blank or matching tests as well as oral presentations or demonstrations, essays, portfolios, and artistic representations of literature, math, science, or social studies concepts.

- Teach test-taking skills by practicing with assessments that use the same format as the statewide tests. Marge could run timed testing sessions, getting ELLs used to working within an extremely limited time frame, beginning with two to three minutes at a time. She could teach students how to eliminate incorrect answers and how to make an informed guess when they aren't sure of the answer.

- Provide timely and clear nonthreatening feedback to ELLs with reference to specific performance criteria that are shared with students before assessments take place. When students know the expectations for their work, they stand a greater chance of meeting them. Marge could give students a checklist that she will use to rate their written essays or oral reports. Students would know exactly what is expected of their performance, assuming Marge has developed a clear and fair checklist of skills.

- Collaborate with colleagues, such as ESL and bilingual education teachers, to plan instruction and assessment that meets the needs of ELLs.

Summary

Recent federal legislation has called attention to the progress of disadvantaged students, including ELLs, in public schools. Elementary, middle, and high school teachers are now to be held accountable for preparing all students to take and demonstrate progress on statewide tests in at least English language arts or reading and mathematics. The new requirements are not without concerns, especially when states set rewards and sanctions for individual students based on standardized test results. States that allow exemptions for ELLs from standardized tests in reading, writing, or the content areas need to provide these students alternate means of assessment in order to be accountable for their progress. ELLs should be included in statewide testing programs through the use of accommodations, alternate assessments, and parental notification.

The validity and reliability of standardized tests used with ELLs as indicators of academic success are questionable since by their status as limited English proficient children, they encounter language and cultural barriers to the content of the tests. Norm-referenced tests are especially inappropriate for making decisions regarding ELLs, and criterion-referenced tests are only useful once students have acquired a level of oral language and literacy in English that allows them to follow test directions and decipher test items. Performance-based assessments offer useful alternatives to norm-referenced and criterion-referenced tests since they can be designed to allow ELLs to show what they can do with what they know and can be more closely aligned with classroom instructional activities.

Results of one-shot, high stakes standardized tests are of little use in help-ing teachers diagnose each student's learning needs and redirect instruction to meet those needs. Using assessment results to improve student learning is critically important in monitoring the progress of ELLs due to the short time frame available for learning English and succeeding in school. However, the kind of information teachers need for identifying the learning needs of ELLs is complex and varied, and such information is not easily found in the results of multiple-choice tests.

Preparing ELLs for statewide testing programs begins in the classroom. Without accurate monitoring of the academic progress of ELLs in general education classrooms, schools cannot realistically expect to prepare these stu-dents for standardized tests.

To help English language learners succeed on state-mandated standard-ized tests, teachers need to begin with their approach to instruction. They can do all of the following:

- Take steps to monitor their students' progress in both English lan-guage development and content area skills and concepts.

- Provide language support as part of instruction and assessment.

- Teach test-taking skills.

- Provide students with clear criteria and feedback that help them meet state standards or local curriculum objectives.

- Collaborate with ESL and bilingual education teachers in providing instruction and assessment for these students.

- Become advocates for a kinder, fairer, and more open system of assessment, for standards-based, criterion-referenced, performance-based assessments and stake a claim at the policy table to influence the development, selection, and use of standardized tests (Calkins, Montgomery, and Santman 1998).

Helping these students succeed must ultimately become a whole school effort. Chapters IV and V will elaborate on what teachers can do through instruction and assessment to help students succeed in school.

IV.

Performance-Based Assessment

All elementary and secondary public school teachers are now charged with improving the academic achievement of English language learners. New federal legislation aims to help disadvantaged minority students succeed in school, and it supports the use of alternative and innovative approaches in the assessment of ELLs. These types of assessments, when designed and used appropriately, can provide valid and reliable measures of progress in English language arts and content area subjects. To help schools fulfill the intent of the new law, classroom teachers will need to monitor the academic and linguistic growth of these ELLs systematically and on an ongoing basis. Recent research has shown that improved assessment practices at the classroom level have beneficial effects on overall achievement, including standardized test scores (Stiggins 2002).

Most assessments used in the classroom are developed by teachers, and these assessments of student work have more influence on instructional decisions than state-mandated tests (Frisby 2001; Wiggins 1998). Yet, very few teachers have had access to the type of assessment information that will enable them to assess English language learners accurately and fairly. In addition, the vast majority of teachers report that they feel unprepared to assess and instruct English language learners (Fradd and Lee 2001). Only about a dozen states require competence in assessment in order to get a teaching license, and the majority of teacher preparation programs fail to provide the kind of education needed for teachers to develop assessments that support student learning (Herman, Aschbacher, and Winters 1992; Stiggins 2002). Most teachers use the same types of tests that were used when they were in school, typically traditional, multiple-choice, fill-in-the-blank, matching, and true/false tests. In fact, little has changed in classroom-based assessment for at least the past fifty years (Bertrand 1994).

Given the limitations of using selected response formats such as multiple-choice tests in assessing ELLs, teachers must look to assessment alternatives for these students. While consensus has yet to be reached on the effectiveness of specific alternatives, many educators are drawn to assessment that is integral to teaching and learning (Marzano, Pickering, and McTighe 1993; Stiggins 2002). This type of assessment can be based on five fundamental assumptions (Harp, 1994; O'Malley & Pierce, 1996; McTighe and Ferrara 1998; Wiggins 1998):

- It must be based on what we know about how language learners learn and how they become readers and writers.

- It is integral to instruction, informs teaching, and improves learning.

- It uses multiple sources of information in a regular and systematic manner.

- It is culturally and developmentally appropriate.

- It provides valid, reliable, and fair measures for redirecting classroom instruction.

Innovative assessment alternatives, such as *performance-based assessment* and *authentic assessment*, hold promise for promoting effective instructional and accurate classroom-based assessment for ELLs. *Performance-based assessment* (PBA) asks students to create or construct a response rather than select a response. By their very nature, performance-based assessments link assessment to instruction and focus on using tasks that are meaningful and engaging to the students. In addition, the primary purpose of these types of assessment is to improve learning. *Authentic assessment* refers to *performance-based assessment* that promotes application of knowledge and skills in situations that closely resemble those of the real world (Frisby 2001; McTighe and Ferrara 1998; Wiggins 1989, 1998). Authentic assessments are potentially more motivating than other types of assessment because they engage students in realistic uses of language and content area concepts.

In this chapter, we look at the benefits of performance-based assessments for ELLs, different types of performance-based assessments, how to attain validity and reliability with teacher-made assessments, how performance-based assessments can be used to support language development and academic achievement, how to adapt assessments for ELLs, and how to overcome some of the challenges in using PBAs.

Why Use Performance-Based Assessment with English Language Learners?

Performance-based approaches to classroom assessment are more appropriate than traditional testing formats for use with English language learners and language minority students for a number of reasons (see Figure 4-1) (Frisby 2001; Hamayan and Damico 1991; O'Malley and Pierce 1996). Used with ELLs, performance-based assessments are more likely than traditional testing formats to:

(1) provide comprehensible input to students

(2) use meaningful, naturalistic context-embedded tasks through hands-on or collaborative activities

(3) show what students know and can do through a variety of assessment tasks

(4) support the language and cognitive needs of ELLs

(5) allow for flexibility in meeting individual needs

(6) use criterion-referenced assessment for judging student work

(7) provide feedback to students on strengths and weaknesses

(8) generate descriptive information that can guide instruction

(9) provide information for teaching and learning that results in improved student performance

What does Performance-Based Assessment for ELLs look like?

Performance-based assessment asks a student to construct a response, create a product, or conduct a demonstration (Feuer and Fulton 1993; Frisby 2001; Herman, Aschbacher, and Winters 1992; McTighe and Ferrara 1998). Constructed responses can be either brief constructed responses (such as open-ended questions, sentence completion items, or graphic organizers) or performance-based assessments. These types of assessments allow more than one correct answer to a problem and typically involve higher-order thinking skills. Performance tasks can also call for integration of language and content area skills. In contrast to standardized or multiple-choice tests that can provide coverage of a wide range of discrete skills, performance-based assessments have the potential for providing in-depth information about a student's ability to integrate knowledge for specific curriculum objectives or standards. Performance-based assessments can be varied and observed and scored as they take place or after the fact (Frisby 2001). PBAs can be one of three types: products, performances, or process-oriented assessments (McTighe and Ferrara 1998). Examples of performance-based assessments that can be useful with ELLs can be found in Figure 4-2 and are described briefly below.

Products are works produced by students that provide concrete examples of their application of knowledge. Some examples are:

- *Writing samples/essays* – Require students to draft a writing sample to meet specified criteria and standards, usually in response to one or more prompts and to be completed in a specified time frame. Allow students to show their mastery of text structures and organization skills, content area concepts, and writing conventions.

- *Projects* – Ask students to collect, analyze, and report information from a number of sources to investigate a content area topic.

- *Art or photo exhibits* – Allow students to show what they know in the content areas through drawings, posters, models, or photographic displays.

- *Portfolios* – Require students to assemble a purposeful collection of work, including drafts, finished products, and self-assessment of progress toward instructional goals.

Performances ask students to demonstrate application of their knowledge and skills under the direct observation of the teacher. A typical example of a performance would be asking a student to show how well he or she can drive a car in order to get a driver's license. Performances can require students to engage in the kinds of tasks that are useful outside of school, such as asking for directions by telephone, demonstrating a process, or arguing a position. All of these can demand high levels of language skill. Examples of performance tasks include:

- *Oral reports* – Allow students to show their effectiveness as oral communicators by reporting on a content area topic using visual aids and real objects.

Figure 4-1
Comparing Traditional to Performance-Based Assessments with English Language Learners

Traditional Assessments (multiple-choice, T/F, matching)	Performance-Based Assessments
Measure skills out of context	Assess learning in contexts meaningful to students
Can provide comprehensible input if choices are provided	Can be designed to provide comprehensible input
Use one or two types of information	Use multiple and varied sources of information
Used at end of unit or chapter	Ongoing and continuous
Indirect measure of language use	Direct measures of real language use
Do not resemble real-life contexts	Similar to real-life contexts
Criteria for performance are typically hidden from students	Make criteria for performance clear to students
Provide limited feedback	Provide specific feedback useful for learning
Only one right answer allowed	No single right answer
Available in textbooks; need time to develop and use	Need time and experience to develop and use

- *Skits/role-plays* – Ask students to use oral language to dramatize a situation or event; can be conducted with puppets, objects, or students as actors.

- *Demonstrations* – Ask students to model or teach a procedure or process to the class.

- *Debates* – Have individual students work with one of two teams to develop and present opposing arguments on a given topic before the class.

Process-Oriented Assessments provide insight into student thinking, reasoning, and motivation. They can provide diagnostic information on how well students use learning strategies. These types of assessments can lead to independent learning by asking students to reflect on their learning and set goals to improve it. Examples are:

- *Think-alouds* – Ask students to verbalize their thinking processes, for example, when reading aloud and making inferences for using context to decipher an unknown word in a reading passage.

- *Self-assessment checklists or surveys* – Promote independent learning and goal setting by asking students to monitor their progress toward standards and instructional goals.

- *Learning logs* – Ask students to analyze prior knowledge and compare it to learning resulting from assigned readings and instructional activities.

- *Individual or pair conferences* – Provide face-to-face opportunities for teachers to interview individuals or pairs of students on attitudes and perceptions of their work and of the learning environment.

- *Teacher observations* – Can be recorded on anecdotal records or other documents; used to note evidence of student progress or lack thereof.

Validity of Performance-Based Assessments in the Classroom

Teachers who develop their own performance-based assessments need to ensure the validity and reliability of these assessments. As discussed in Chapter III, when an assessment task accurately measures student learning on the curriculum and instructional objectives being monitored (and which have been presented to students in the classroom), it can be said to have ***content validity***. This alignment between instruction and assessment provides the basis for the content validity of the assessment. To assess skills or knowledge

Figure 4-2
Menu of Performance-Based Assessments for ELLs

Completion	Product	Performance	Process-Oriented
Sentence completion	Writing sample/essay	Oral report	Think-aloud
Short answer	Project	Skit or role-play	Self-assessment checklist or survey
Label a diagram or picture	Art or photo exhibit	Demonstration	Individual or pair conference
Graphic Organizers	Portfolio	Debate	Literature response journal
• Webs			
• Outlines			
• Drawings			Teacher observation
• Tables/charts			

Adapted from McTighe and Ferrara, 1998

not presented in class would result in diminished content validity. Wiggins (1998) offers two useful questions to ask to determine the validity of performance-based assessment tasks:

(1) Could the student *do well* on the task for reasons that have little to do with the desired understanding or skill being assessed?

(2) Could the student *do poorly* on the task for reasons that have little to do with the desired understanding or skill?

If the answer to either question above is *yes*, the assessment results will lack validity.

An example of an assessment task that lacks content validity would be evaluating the ability of a high school ELL to prepare a research paper in world history when the student has not yet had instruction in writing a research paper.

Consequential validity requires that teachers use the results of their daily or weekly assessments to improve the effectiveness of their teaching as well as to improve student learning. All too often, teachers, believing that more is better, collect more assessment data than they can use for making judgments either about student learning or about the effectiveness of their lessons. Consequential validity would be better served if teachers conducted fewer, more purposeful assessments and used the results of student performance for redirecting their teaching and subsequently improving student learning. For example, teachers often say that they have "covered" certain objectives in class but that students have not "learned" them yet. To obtain consequential validity, teachers need to examine priority standards or objectives to be mastered by ELLs and present activities for learning these in a number of different ways that provide comprehensible input, until the students make progress on the objectives. Providing specific, descriptive (rather than judgmental) feedback to students on ways to improve their performance can also add consequential validity to assessments.

As discussed in Chapter III, the validity of any assessment can be threatened by the presence of bias. Teachers using performance-based assessment in the classroom with ELLs need to be aware of their own bias in judging students and their work. Bias can be of several types: (1) cultural bias (assuming prior knowledge and experiences are the same for ELLs as for all other students), (2) assessment bias (expecting ELLs to have the same rules as native speakers of English for working independently, for cheating, and for working within specified time limits), and (3) norming bias (comparing the progress of ELLs to that of native speakers of English). McTighe and Ferrara (1998) add another type of bias, the "halo and pitchfork effect." Expectations for student work are set based on previous attitudes, behavior, or performance, and great deviations from that range of grading or achievement are not anticipated. To avoid these effects, teachers can use blind scoring of student work by removing each student's name from his or her work and assigning an identification code. Returning to review the work at a later time can help distance the work itself from the identity of the author. Using a scoring rubric or checklist can also help assess students' work objectively rather than against previous performance.

Reliability of Performance-Based Assessments in the Classroom

Classroom-based, teacher-made assessments have typically received a less than favorable reputation for being subjective. Unlike standardized and multiple-choice test items, which have a single answer (it is either right or wrong), performance-based assessments have more than one correct answer and require teacher judgment in scoring. Introducing the element of professional judgment results in a high likelihood that scoring will vary between teachers and that teachers will assign scores on the basis of differing criteria. Teacher grading policies and the different work samples and performances graded by each teacher are also variable and can produce inconsistencies in teacher judgment. To build increased reliability for their own performance-based assessments, teachers can take a few simple steps:

- First, to establish *intra-rater reliability*, or consistency of an individual teacher in applying a single set of criteria to multiple samples of student work (for example, a pile of essays), teachers can use multiple and varied measures and develop scoring criteria for the most important performance tasks and work samples that students produce. Rather than compare the work of ELLs to native speakers of English, teachers can monitor student progress relative to a standard in the form of a criterion for performance. Using criterion-referenced assessment is a much more fair and equitable way to evaluate the work of ELLs than other types of assessment involving the comparison of these students to other groups of students. Clearly specified scoring criteria in the form of checklists or scoring rubrics can help ensure that teachers are evaluating each student's work along the same standards, not having higher expectations for some students than for others. Criteria may take the form of holistic or analytic scoring rubrics, rating scales, teacher observation checklists, or other assessment tools (see Chapter V).

- *Inter-rater reliability* can be attained by enlisting one or more teachers to rate a student's work or performance. Inter-rater reliability is especially important in the case of high-stakes decision making (such as placement in or out of a Title I or ESL program). When in doubt, teachers can consult colleagues to see if they agree on a student's score. Inter-rater reliability, or agreement between raters, can be established by discussing how to apply scoring criteria consistently and through the use of **anchor papers** or **performances** (representative samples of student work at each score point). A high degree of inter-rater reliability would mean that raters reach consensus on student scores the majority of the time. Agreement between raters at least 80 percent of the time would be good inter-rater reliability according to Herman et al, 1992. An example of multiple teacher-raters attaining agreement on student work can be found in the development and application of scoring rubrics for writing by teachers. The author had between 5 and 15 teachers each score independently over 80 writing samples produced by ELLs at elementary, middle, and secondary school levels. In the process, we found that we improved the clarity of the language and the accuracy of the scoring rubric and were able to identify anchor papers at each score point with a high level of inter-rater reliability (about 90 percent).

Developmental vs. Absolute Standards

In some cases, it is appropriate to set different standards for individual students, especially in the case of students with learning or emotional disabilities or where classrooms display a wide range of English language proficiency and cognitive ability. When teachers use standards appropriate to each student's current level of ability, they are using **developmental** or **relative standards.** When all students must meet the same standards, teachers are applying **absolute standards**. An example of an absolute standard in science could be:

The student will investigate and understand that objects can be described in terms of the materials they are made of and their physical properties. Key concepts include: objects are made of smaller parts; materials are composed of parts that are too small to be seen without magnification; and physical properties remain the same as the material is reduced in size (Virginia Standards of Learning, Grade 3 Science 1995).

Teachers of ELLs will need to adapt absolute standards for individual students that reflect their current level of English language proficiency and cognitive development to facilitate teaching and learning. Rather than expect ALL students to meet the same performance standard, teachers can set developmental standards for each student or for groups of students, depending on their strengths and needs. For example, in a mixed-ability classroom, beginners (ELLs with one or two years of English language instruction) would be expected to progress at a rate of learning and to master language features different from those to be mastered by an advanced language learner. Similarly, an intermediate or advanced ELL might attain high standards in oral language and not reach performance levels in writing set for native English-speaking peers. What is important is that each ELL make progress toward the absolute standards, even if it is at a slower pace than that of native speakers of English (see Chapter II for a description of how long it takes to learn another language for school). An example of assessment using developmental standards for the science standard described above might look like this:

For beginning ELLs (typically those who have received one or two years of English language instruction)—The student will **describe orally or make a diagram or graphic organizer to show** how objects are made of smaller parts.

For intermediate English language learners (having received three or more years of English language instruction)—The student will **complete an outline** describing materials that are composed of parts too small to be seen without magnification. The student will **demonstrate** how physical properties of matter remain the same even when the material is reduced in size.

Three Approaches to Adapting Assessments for ELLs

The promise of innovative approaches to assessing the performance of ELLs lies primarily in the flexibility and fairness they offer in measuring and responding to student learning. Nevertheless, to take into account the language proficiency status of ELLs, teachers will need to make modifications to

Figure 4-3
Scaffolding Assessments by Language Proficiency Level

English Language Proficiency Level / Scaffolding Approaches	Beginner	Interm	Advanced
1. **Simplify language** (reduce sentence length, use present tense only, enlarge font size)	✔	✔	✔
2. **Simplify format** (reduce number of items, remove distracting graphics, cut into smaller chunks or tasks)	✔	✔	
3. **Tap prior knowledge/personal experience** (e.g., pre-reading, pre-writing strategies)	✔	✔	✔
4. **Add meaningful visuals, graphic organizers to task or question**	✔	✔	✔
5. **Allow an oral, pictorial, or physical response** (e.g., gestures, illustrations)	✔	✔	
6. **Complete an outline, T-list, or semantic map**	✔	✔	✔
7. **Complete, given a list, examples, or sentence stem**	✔	✔	✔
8. **Provide vocabulary lists or glossary**	✔	✔	
9. **Label parts or functions**	✔	✔	✔
10. **Select from several options** (e.g., word bank)	✔	✔	✔
11. **Make a list of attributes**		✔	✔
12. **Use cooperative learning/ collaborative tasks**	✔	✔	✔
13. **Modeling by teacher**	✔	✔	✔
14. **Show model performances**	✔	✔	✔
15. **Use manipulatives**			
16. **Use music, drama, role-play, puppets**	✔	✔	✔
17. **Ask for evidence to support response**		✔	✔
18. **Read items aloud to student**	✔		
19. **Use native language**	✔		
20. **Use taped directions**	✔	✔	

performance-based assessments they may already use with native speakers of English. Teachers can use three approaches for adapting assessments for ELLs: *scaffolding, visible criteria,* and *differentiated scoring.* These three approaches can help ensure that teachers evaluate student work fairly and consistently and provide ELLs with the linguistic support and feedback they need to improve their learning.

Scaffolding, an essential approach to adapting assessments for ELLs, entails providing language support so that the language of the assessment does not become an obstacle to a student's showing content area knowledge. Scaffolding has as its primary purpose the providing of comprehensible input through the use of temporary linguistic supports that reduce the language load on a students' ability to demonstrate his or her understanding through English.

Commonly used scaffolding approaches are useful for all at-risk learners. Assessment tasks or prompts are modified and student response modes are expanded from traditional formats. Teachers can modify the assessment task by simplifying the language and the format (many teacher-made assessments are too wordy and can overwhelm English language learners because they do not provide comprehensible input), providing word banks or other clues to responses, using visuals or graphics to present the task, and modeling the task for students. Scaffolding approaches can allow students to respond by choosing from options for tasks and responses, using visuals or graphic organizers and/or manipulatives, and by working with partners. For a list of some commonly used scaffolding approaches, see Figure 4-3.

To support language development, scaffolding asks students to complete information that is already partially provided (rather than generate from scratch on a blank piece of paper), as in completion of a partially completed outline, table, or paragraph. Examples of assessments with and without scaffolded prompts are presented in Figure 4-4. For an example of an end-of-unit assessment on insects for elementary students before and after scaffolding, see Figures 4-5 and 4-6.

Teachers use *visible criteria* when they share their expectations for student work and performance in as explicit terms as possible using a scoring rubric, checklist, or other assessment tool. This approach is especially important with ELLs, who have been shown to benefit from the teacher's sharing of

Figure 4-4
Assessment with Scaffolded Prompts

Sample prompt	Without Scaffolding	With Scaffolding
Explain a content area concept	Write a one-page essay explaining what democracy means	Write a list of the features of DEMOCRACY and briefly describe each
Summarize a text or assigned reading	Write a paragraph summary of the concept of condensation, include at least 3 main ideas	Complete an outline or graphic organizer describing condensation or explain it orally
Write a word problem	Create a problem for probability; give equation, problem, and question	Complete a word problem on probability given examples and an outline of a sample problem
Write up a science lab report	Write a report of procedures used in a science experiment on the digestive system	Complete a summary report given an outline or list of steps and vocabulary items used in the experiment or use a graphic organizer such as a flow chart or table.

Adapted from O'Malley and Pierce, 1996

Figure 4-5

End-of-Unit Test on Insects: Without Scaffolding

Unit Test: *Insects*

Part I

1. Describe the life cycle of each of the following:

    - Monarch butterfly

    - Mantis

    - Honeybee

2. What foods do most insects eat?

3. Describe the anatomy and habitat of the grasshopper.

4. How do honeybees make honey?

5. Why are insects important?

the assessment criteria in advance of the assessment itself (Kolls 1992). When teachers share their expectations with students in vague or general terms, students are less able to meet them. However, when teachers state these expectations in terms of specific outcomes in language the students can understand, and by showing them examples of excellent work, the likelihood of their attaining the criteria is greatly increased (McTighe and Ferrara 1998; O'Malley and Pierce 1996; Stiggins 2002). (See examples of scoring rubrics and checklists in Chapter V.)

Teachers need to model for students how they will apply the standards or criteria to their work by demonstrating with samples of student work in class. It is probably best to use examples from students in previous classes or those who are not currently enrolled in the class. If such work is not available, teachers would be well advised to get permission from students to use their work for demonstration in class.

Differentiated scoring is the determination of separate scores for one assignment, one score for language and the other for content area subject matter. With differentiated scoring, teachers can more fairly assess each student's strengths in both content area knowledge and English language proficiency. Differentiated scores also provide specific feedback to students on what they can do well and what they need to continue to work on, and this can build self-confidence and motivation for learning. For example, an ELL submitting a lab report in earth science could be assigned two scores for the report: one for the process and content learning in science and another for ability to communicate through written English. This avoids confounding language skills with content area knowledge.

Many teachers might feel uncomfortable assigning a high grade or score to a lab report that shows accurate content area knowledge but weak writing skills. They might judge the entire report on the level of writing only. By using differentiated scoring, a teacher can assign separate scores that give the student credit for science knowledge while also suggesting that he or she work on writing skills. For grading purposes, rather than averaging scores, teachers can assign a weight to each score (such as 40 percent of total grade) and add the scores to calculate a grade for the assignment. For an example of a differentiated scoring rubric for a science journal, see Figure 4-7.

Figure 4-6
End-of-Unit Assessment on Insects: With Scaffolding
(Partially Completed Graphic Organizer)

Data Retrieval Chart

Name	Life Cycle	Food	Habitat	Anatomy	Importance	Other Interesting Facts
Monarch Butterfly	Complete meta-morphosis Egg Larva Pupa (chrysalis) Adult butterfly	Egg (for larva) Milkweed leaves (larva) Nectar from flowers (for adult)	N. & S. America, Asia, Australia Hawaiian Islands Parts of Europe Flowers, Milk-weed plants	Hood eyes, antenna, jaws thorax (legs & 4 wings) abdomen	Adult butterflies drink nectar, aid in pollination (fertilization) of flowers	Can fly up to 2000 miles to migrate Do not fly at night
Mantis						
Honeybees						

Adapted from Clemmons & Laase, 1995

Peer- and Self-Assessment

As for any student, an important aspect of performance-based assessment for ELLs is its potential for actively engaging students in evaluating their own work. Peer- and self-assessment are essential for teaching students how to manage their own study habits and use of learning strategies and how to reflect on progress toward learning goals. The goal of self-assessment is to produce students who can learn independently of the teacher. To accomplish this, teachers need to help each student recognize his or her individual responsibility for learning. Self-assessment also plays a role in motivating learners to continue learning and building self-confidence in their ability to learn.

Teachers who have learned how to teach self- and peer-assessment techniques can teach even young children to evaluate their own work with regard to pre-established criteria. For example, teachers of primary ESL students in one elementary school have taught their second and third graders to evaluate their own work using portfolio assessment. In another school system, an elementary teacher has added graphics and rebus-like statements to a student self-assessment learning log of reading comprehension; she has developed an assessment tool that provides comprehensible input for her young learners while also promoting self-confidence in their ability to learn.

Critical elements in teaching self-assessment to ELLs are teacher modeling and scaffolding, both in instruction and assessment. ELLs need many opportunities to see teachers model expected performance and application of assessment criteria before they can be expected to apply the guidelines to their own work. Involving ELLs in whole class criteria-setting for important tasks can also help students become independent evaluators of their own work and the work of others.

Beginning ELLs may not be capable of expressing self-evaluation in English, and providing these students with options through scaffolding and/or use of the native language to reflect on their work may help get them started in evaluating that work. Teachers can ask other students who are bilingual in the language of the beginner to translate their self-assessment.

Teachers who want to begin using self- and peer-assessment with ELLs will need to examine their approach to teaching. Teachers who already use carefully structured, purposeful cooperative learning activities will have an easier

Figure 4-7
Differentiated Scoring in Science (Drafting a Scoring Rubric)

RATING	LANGUAGE	SCIENCE CONCEPTS
4	Uses own language to paraphrase and describe what is read. Writes with appropriate word order and sentence formation. Uses well-formed paragraphs. Makes few grammatical/mechanical errors, and these do not interfere with meaning.	Applies prior knowledge and makes a personal response to what is read. Addresses content area concepts accurately with few or no misconceptions. Uses content area vocabulary wherever it applies. Uses reading strategies such as summarizing and making inferences.
3	Uses own language for partial paraphrasing and describing what is read. Writes with some errors in word order and sentence formation. Develops paragraphs that need improved organization. May make a number of grammatical/mechanical errors, but these do not interfere with meaning.	Applies prior knowledge but may make a limited personal response to what is read. Addresses content area concepts with some inaccuracies. Uses content area vocabulary in some instances but not all. Uses a limited number of reading strategies such as summarizing and making inferences.
2		
1		

55

time of pairing students to work with partners for peer feedback than those who do not. For other teachers, it may take additional modeling and reinforcement of student roles and responsibilities. For students to assess a peer's work and their own work it will be necessary to help ELLs become comfortable with these types of assessment.

A Balanced Approach to Assessment

To be able to collect accurate information about ELLs, teachers need to use a variety of assessments that range from multiple-choice tests of basic skills to performance-based assessments. Generalizability of assessment results is key (Fradd and Lee 2001; Herman, Aschbacher, and Winters 1992; Stiggins 2002). Can the results of the assessments be used to make inferences and generalizations about the student's understanding, skills, and strategies? Do the skills that the student uses in the assessment context transfer to other situations and problems? Teachers can help increase the achievement of ELLs by taking a balanced approach to assessment; using assessment tasks and tools that match a specified purpose; using a variety of assessment tasks and tools on an ongoing basis; providing specific feedback to students on how they can improve their performance; holding high expectations for them; and providing them with challenging content area materials and tasks. Performance-based assessments can be time-consuming to develop, observe, and evaluate, especially for teachers and students who are new to the process and for the teacher working alone. PBAs can be less time-consuming to develop when produced in collaboration with a colleague or in teacher teams.

Summary

Marge Smith has tried using the same end-of-unit, multiple-choice and completion tests with the English language learners in her class as she uses with the rest of her students. Each time the ELLs have failed. Sometimes, she has found them to be copying or at least giving each other the answers. All she knows now is what they cannot do. She wonders how she can find out what they do know so that she can help them build their learning on that knowledge.

Teachers who want to find out how well ELLs understand and process content area subjects need to make assessments accessible to them. They can do this by reducing the language barrier that serves as an obstacle to ELLs showing what they know. Teachers can also use other types of assessments besides paper-and-pencil tests with ELLs. Performance-based and brief constructed response assessments that are carefully designed with scaffolding for ELLs can serve as useful alternatives to traditional testing formats for instructional feedback toward getting each student to mastery.

To help schools meet the intent of new federal accountability requirements, teachers will need to use improved assessment practices in the classroom. Improved assessment practices, which have been linked to the performance standards are integral to instruction and have as their purpose the improvement of student attainment of the state standards.

Scoring Tools

Teachers using performance-based assessments for monitoring the progress of English language learners in their classrooms will want to develop scoring tools to support the assessment tasks. Once assessment tasks are designed, teachers can individually or in teams design the scoring criteria and tools for each task. Because constructed-response formats allow more than one possible answer, teachers will need to use criterion-referenced scoring tools to evaluate student responses. These scoring tools can demonstrate student mastery of state and local standards or curriculum objectives with more sensitivity than traditional norm-referenced tests. This chapter suggests approaches for eliciting student responses on assessment tasks and provides an overview of several approaches to scoring performance-based assessment tasks with English language learners.

Useful Prompting Techniques

Teachers who are skilled in working with English language learners use a number of approaches for eliciting responses from them. These approaches or prompting techniques serve to bring prior knowledge (e.g., of previous lessons, readings, or world knowledge) to bear on the learning of new content information. As discussed in Chapter IV, the teacher can provide scaffolding (reducing the language load) to assessment questions and tasks in order to show ELLs that they can perform the tasks required of them. Prompting techniques include:

- *Making personal connections with concepts.* Teachers may ask students what in their personal experience relates to the topic of study, use current events or common daily experiences relating to the topic, or give an example from their own experience to make the topic meaningful for ELLs.

- *Providing categories for classification.* Categories given as prompts help learners see relationships between concepts and can make the performance task less intimidating. Once ELLs recognize the categories, they can search for answers in textbooks or other learning materials. Examples might be graphic organizers such as tables or charts with categories listed across the top and side, timelines with years indicated, or semantic webs with key topics indicated (see examples in Chapter IV). Teachers could also use photographs or drawings to stimulate and motivate verbal and written responses from ELLs and to tap prior knowledge.

- *Modeling and showing in writing.* Teachers can model for students by working through examples of expected performance with the whole class, using think-alouds to relate their thinking processes, and writing key words and phrases on the board or projector.

Types of Scoring Tools

Constructed response formats include brief constructed responses, student performances or demonstrations of understanding, student products, and process-oriented assessments. These types of assessment yield a wide range of responses from students and depend on teachers exercising their judgment about the merit of student work against a set of carefully specified criteria in the form of scoring tools.

Four categories of scoring tools that can be used for evaluating the work of English language learners are checklists, scoring rubrics, rating scales, and teacher observations (written and oral comments) (Herman, Aschbacher, and Winters, 1992; McTighe and Ferrara, 1998; O'Malley and Pierce, 1996). These scoring tools, commonly used to rate performance assessments, have both advantages and disadvantages:

Checklists. Behaviors or skills observed by the teacher can be listed for each student. Lists are useful for marking whether or not a student exhibits a desired behavior or whether a skill is present, such as steps in the writing process or a science experiment or skills and strategies required in the reading process. Lists, which are relatively simple to use and not as time-consuming to complete as other assessment tools, can also be used with English language learners for self-assessment. Figure 5-1 provides a checklist for students' use of graphic organizers in assessment of reading comprehension. Figure 5-2 is a checklist developed by an English Language Arts/ESOL teacher for monitoring students' writing skills at the paragraph level.

- Advantages—Checklists can indicate what ELLs can do and show progress on discrete skills or processes. They are useful for communicating with parents or other teachers.

- Limitation—They cannot be used for describing a range of skills or quality of performance.

Figure 5-1

Checklist for Graphic Organizers

Name_____ Date_____

1. _____ Identifies main ideas accurately

2. _____ Provides details and examples

3. _____ Omits extraneous information

4. _____ Shows connections between concepts

5. _____ Uses appropriate graphic organizer

6. _____ Discusses with others the elements of a graphic organizer

7. _____ Modifies graphic organizer after reading

8. _____ Explains graphic organizer orally or in writing

Figure 5-2

Self-Assessment Writing Checklist
Grades 7-8, Intermediate English Language Learners

Name_____ Date_____

This is a checklist for your FINAL DRAFT.

How to use this checklist:

1. Read your paragraph carefully **at least twice.**
2. Put a check ✔ if you can respond YES to any item about your writing.
3. Put an X if your answer is NO to any item.
4. Where you have NO, **EDIT and REVISE** those parts of your writing.

A. Organization
My paragraph has:
_____1. a topic sentence.

_____2. a body with three supporting details.

_____3. examples to explain each detail.

_____4. a closing sentence.

_____5. sentences in sequential order.

B. Content
My paragraph:
_____6. starts in an interesting way.

_____7. is easy to read and understand.

C. Grammar & Mechanics
My paragraph has:
_____8. appropriate spelling.

_____9. standard grammar.

_____10. required punctuation.

D. Your goals
I need to improve my paragraph in these ways:

_____

_____

Scoring Rubrics. Fixed scales with descriptions of performance are provided for each level or score point.

- *Holistic rubrics* assign a single score to an entire student product or performance. They are recommended for summative (end-of-unit or project) assessments as well as for complex or multiple component tasks such as research projects, oral presentations, and essays. (See Figure 5-3 for an example of a holistic scoring rubric for teacher use in monitoring the writing growth of ELLs in middle and high school).

- *Primary trait scoring* focuses on evidence of a particular trait or feature that has been emphasized in instruction, such as the use of technical vocabulary or a research protocol. This type of scoring can be especially useful with English language learners in that it provides direct and specific feedback on only one aspect of learning at a time. Figure 5-4 shows a primary trait scoring rubric to be used by teachers with beginning and intermediate level writers.

  - Advantages—Primary trait scoring is useful for determining the progress of ELLs along a continuum.

  - Disadvantages—This scoring method does not indicate specific areas of strength and weakness in language and content.

- *Analytic rubrics* give separate scores to various aspects of a single assignment.

  - Advantages—Analytic rubrics are useful with ELLs for diagnosing specific areas of strength and weakness in language or content. They can be used for daily or weekly assignments to provide feedback to students and to redirect instruction.

  - Disadvantages—They can be time-consuming to develop and use.

Figure 5-3

Holistic Scoring Rubric for Writing
Grades 6-12

To receive a particular score, a writing sample MUST meet the criteria described in all lines of bold type plus two additional criteria at a given score point.

Level 5
- **Addresses the prompt thoroughly.**
- **Presents a clear topic sentence and develops a central idea using multiple paragraphs with clear introduction, details, and effective use of transitions.**
- **Has few errors in usage, and these do not interfere with meaning.**
- Writes with a variety of sentence structures and clear evidence of writer's voice.
- Uses a variety of descriptive vocabulary.
- Has few errors in mechanics and/or spelling.

Level 4
- **Addresses the prompt but may contain unrelated details.**
- **Presents a clear topic sentence and develops a central idea in a coherent paragraph with limited use of transitions.**
- Has some errors in usage, but these do not interfere with meaning.
- Uses simple, compound, and/or complex sentences with some evidence of writer's voice.
- Uses limited descriptive vocabulary that may be repetitive.
- Has some errors in mechanics and/or spelling.

Level 3
- **May not address the prompt.**
- **Presents a central idea using multiple related sentences that lack paragraph structure.**
- **Has a variety of errors in usage, and these may interfere with meaning.**
- Uses simple and/or compound sentences.
- Uses vocabulary ineffectively and repetitively.
- Has many errors in mechanics and/or spelling, including run-on sentences and sentence fragments.

Level 2
- **Presents or lists one or more ideas that may be related but lacks organizational structure.**
- **Has consistent errors in usage, and these interfere with meaning.**
- Uses phrases and/or simple and compound sentences.
- Uses repetitive vocabulary.
- Has many errors in mechanics and/or spelling.

Level 1
- **Uses letter strings, symbols, or pictures to convey meaning.**
- Writes single words, copies from a model, and may use native language.
- Shows little evidence of mechanics and/or standard spelling.

Figure 5-4

Primary Trait Scoring Rubric for Writing

Focus: Central Idea Development
Grade Level: 9-11
Level of English Proficiency: Beginner and Intermediate

Score	Criterion
6	Fully develops central idea and elaborates with details and examples.
5	Develops central idea partially with supporting details and examples.
4	Supports a central idea with some relevant details.
3	Writes multiple sentences around a central idea with a series of related ideas.
2	Writes complete, incomplete, or pattern sentences.
1	Uses single words, phrases, or native language or draws or copies from a model.

Figure 5-5 shows an example of an analytic rubric for assessment of writing. Figure 5-6 provides an example of an analytic rubric for an oral report on a research project. Both rubrics have been designed for teacher (rather than student) use.

Figure 5-5
Analytic Scoring Rubric for Writing, Grades 6-12

DOMAIN SCORE	PROMPT	ORGANIZATION	USAGE (GRAMMAR)	SENTENCE STRUCTURE	VOCABULARY	MECHANICS/ SPELLING
5	Addresses the prompt thoroughly.	Presents a clear topic sentence and develops a central idea using multiple paragraphs with clear introduction, details, and effective use of transitions.	Has few errors in usage, and these do not interfere with meaning.	Writes with a variety of sentence structures and clear evidence of writer's voice.	Uses a variety of descriptive vocabulary.	Has few errors in mechanics and/or spelling.
4	Addresses the prompt but may contain unrelated details.	Presents a clear topic sentence and develops a central idea in a coherent paragraph with limited use of transitions.	Has some errors in usage, but these do not interfere with meaning.	Uses simple, compound, and/or complex sentences with some evidence of writer's voice.	Uses limited descriptive vocabulary that may be repetitive.	Has some errors in mechanics and/or spelling.
3	May not address the prompt.	Presents a central idea using multiple related sentences that lack paragraph structure.	Has a variety of errors in usage, and these may interfere with meaning.	Uses simple and/or compound sentences.	Uses vocabulary ineffectively and repetitively.	Has many errors in mechanics and/or spelling, including run-on sentences and sentence fragments.
2	May not address the prompt.	Presents or lists one or more ideas that may be related but lacks organizational structure.	Has consistent errors in usage, and these interfere with meaning.	Uses phrases and/or simple and compound sentences.	Uses repetitive vocabulary.	Has many errors in mechanics and/or spelling.
1	May not address the prompt.	Lacks organizational structure.	Uses letter strings, symbols, or pictures to convey meaning.	Writes single words or copies from a model.	May use native language.	Shows little evidence of mechanics and/or standard spelling.

Figure 5-6

Animal Research Project—Oral Presentation and Powerpoint Slide Show

Domain Score	Quality of Information	Use of a variety of sources	Oral Presentation	Slide Show	Language Skills
4	Describes all aspects of animal's life accurately.	Uses more than 3 sources of information.	Presents well-organized report.	Makes effective use of space on each slide, of graphics, and of equipment.	Speaks clearly and fluently with few errors in vocabulary or grammar.
3	Describes animal's life incompletely or with some inaccuracies.	Uses at least 3 sources of information.	Presents report with some lack of organization.	Uses space on slides ineffectively, uses few graphics, or has problems, or has problems with equipment.	Speaks audibly and has errors in vocabulary or grammar.
2	Describes few aspects of animal's life or with many inaccuracies.	Uses two sources of information.	Presents report with minimum organization.	Uses space on slides ineffectively and uses few graphics or has problems with equipment.	Speaks inaudibly or has numerous errors in grammar and/or vocabulary.
1	Describes few aspects of animal's life.	Uses one source of information.	Presents report with no apparent organization.	Uses space on slides ineffectively, uses few graphics and has problems with equipment.	Speaks inaudibly, with hesitations, or with numerous errors in grammar and/or vocabulary.

Animal research project using a variety of sources, including textbooks, trade books, encyclopedias, magazines, the Internet.

In designing scoring rubrics, teachers need to keep in mind that the number of **score points** used will affect the reliability of the outcomes. The larger the number of points, the less reliability there will be. This is because the wider the spread between the major score points, the harder it is to distinguish between those score points with any degree of consistency. For assessing English language learners, a longer scale will allow teachers to make finer distinctions in performance than a shorter scale. If teachers want to decide who needs additional help on learning objectives, a scoring rubric with several points should be feasible to use in a limited time frame.

Teachers should not use 100-point scales—based on the notion of percentages, as in 100 percent correct—to assign grades for student work because of the interferences of subjectivity and teacher bias involved in determining other student grades using this approach.

Rubrics ideally should also be accompanied by *anchors* or examples of performance at each score point on a rubric. One way to model teacher expectations for performance is through anchor papers or performances (such as videotaped oral reports). Providing rubrics and other scoring tools to students for explaining performance criteria is a useful beginning, but without anchor papers and performances, English language learners may not clearly understand the nature of the task.

Rating scales are useful for questionnaires and surveys of student interest or for peer- and self-assessment. They can provide effective comprehensible input and elicit personal responses from ELLs. Figure 5-7 shows an example of a rating scale for self-assessment in social studies.

- Advantages—Rating scales show a range of performance on a fixed scale for a number of different categories.
- Disadvantages—Ratings can be vague or subjective.

Teacher Observations

Written and oral comments in the form of anecdotal records or student/teacher conferences are useful for providing students and parents with details on the quality and range of student learning. For English language learners, anecdotal records and conferences can be effective for providing personalized feedback on each student's strengths and needs in learning. To achieve accurate feedback, however, teachers' comments need to address spe-

Figure 5-7

Rating Scale for Self-Assessment in Social Studies

Grade 8, Intermediate ELLs

How do you feel about social studies?

Circle ONE answer for each statement below.

Statement	Agree	Not sure	Disagree
1. I like to learn in social studies class.	1	2	3
2. Before I read, I think about what I already know on the topic.	1	2	3
3. I understand most of what I read.	1	2	3
4. I take notes or draw pictures to remember important information.	1	2	3
5. I connect topics to my life experiences.	1	2	3
6. I reread sentences before and after a word I do not know.	1	2	3
7. I am happy with my grades and work in social studies class.	1	2	3

8. Other comments:

cific elements of quality in student work in comparison to standards or criteria and must make positive, concrete suggestions for improvement.

Caveats

Several cautions need to be observed when using performance-based assessment tools with English language learners. Teachers should be careful not to judge the performance of ELLs against that of their monolingual English-speaking peers. Teachers may also want to be wary of:

- Basing assessment tools on past experiences with native speakers of English (not English language learners) to assess the performance of ELLs; the tool will not be valid or reliable.

- Stating that a student is reading on a "third-grade level" or "below grade level". In this case, the performance of English language learners is being compared to an inexact measure of learning for native speakers of English rather than to a particular standard or criterion of mastery.

- Grading on the curve, in which students are assigned a grade based on a certain percentage of the class getting A's, another percentage getting B's, and so on. Not only is grading on the curve inappropriate for English language learners, it is also unfair and statistically incorrect when used with students in small numbers, as in classroom settings.

- Using the same assessment format routinely with both native speakers of English and English language learners. A combination of various assessment formats, when used appropriately, can provide valid and reliable feedback to English language learners.

Summary

Marge Smith teaches middle school earth science using state standards as her guide. She has students read a variety of texts, conduct lab experiments, and produce oral and written reports. She has begun using graphic organizers (semantic webs, flow charts, tables) and other visual aides to help the English language learners in her class understand the concepts presented. Since the ELLs in her class are not yet proficient in oral or written English, she will also use their individual completion of graphic organizers to judge what they have learned from the books and in-class presentations about various types of rocks (she is actually using this approach with all the students in her class). She can use a checklist to focus on specific elements of comprehension represented on the graphic organizers (e.g., main ideas, details) that have been taught in class. In this way, she can more easily identify her ELL students' areas of strength and weakness.

Teachers developing their own performance-based assessment tools for monitoring the growth of English language learners will need ways to elicit student responses and to score those responses. To elicit student responses, teachers can use prompting techniques that ensure that students are making personal connections with the concepts being presented, see the relationships between concepts, and can base their work on whole-class demonstrations. Teacher modeling is an essential part of instruction and assessment in the content areas; providing examples of student work through anchor papers and works is another.

In scoring the performance of English language learners, teachers can choose from, among other assessment tools, checklists, scoring rubrics, rating scales, and oral and written teacher comments. A combination of various assessment activities and formats can provide valid and reliable information to the teacher and feedback to the learner with regard to progress in the content area classroom.

Note:

The author expresses her appreciation for the contributions of many teachers to the development of the materials contained in the figures in this chapter. These teachers have participated in workshops that she has conducted in recent years. They adapted and modified existing materials and in some cases created original materials. Specifically, appreciation is expressed to the following:

Kate Kraiwan
Nicole Lutz
Pelin Rau
Barbara Rose
Prince William County (VA) ESOL Writing Assessment Team

VI.

Professional Development

Research has shown that improvements in classroom-based assessment can help increase the overall achievement of minority students and raise their standardized test scores (Stiggins 1998). Therefore, teachers who want to have a positive effect on the achievement of English language learners will want to learn more about assessment approaches that serve this purpose. Professional development opportunities can provide access to needed information and skills in this area. Furthermore, the highest quality professional development activities have as their goal the improvement of the achievement of students from diverse cultural and socioeconomic backgrounds (National Foundation for the Improvement of Education, 1996). This chapter outlines a process for getting started with professional development, from building a team to revising the assessments. This process has been adapted from Baker (1993), Herman, Aschbacher, and Winters (1992), and O'Malley and Pierce (1996).

Step 1: Build a Team

To begin, teachers need to create an assessment study team or focus group of teachers and administrators interested in improving the academic achievement of English language learners. A collaborative approach between mainstream and ESOL or bilingual education teachers would likely yield the most fruitful approach to developing appropriate assessment tasks and tools for English language learners.

This step is critical, because the success or failure of the professional development initiative will depend on the makeup of each team. It is not necessary to involve all teachers in a school or district in the professional development program. However, it is highly desirable to call for interested volunteers and then to select from this pool those who:

(1) are willing to make a serious time commitment both collaboratively and through individual study and reflection;

(2) have some experience working with ELLs or culturally diverse populations;

(3) have shown positive attitudes in implementing innovations in their own practice; and

(4) collaborate easily with others.

Each team member should be willing to make a time commitment of at least one year to work with the study team.

Teachers work together in self-selected teams to develop assessment tasks and tools for improving the achievement of ELLs based on research and practice. These teams can be formed by grade level or range (e.g., Grades 1-3, 4-8, 9-12) and by content area (mathematics, science, social studies). For example, upper elementary teachers may want to work together to develop assessment activities and tools for instructional units based on standards in social studies dealing with knowledge about early Americans. Teams are collegial and experimental; teachers are free to create, adapt, and try out activities that have shown promise with ELLs. The ultimate goal is to develop materials that will improve the learning of ELLs and that can be used to benefit all students in a classroom.

Step 2: Determine the Purpose

Teachers must determine a primary purpose for the assessments to be developed. Is it to improve the achievement of English language learners in reading? In writing? In science? Purposes can range from monitoring student progress in the classroom to placement in instructional programs. One way to determine the purpose is to survey teachers regarding their need for information and skills in assessing English language learners.

Data gathering for determining assessment purpose can be conducted through a needs assessment consisting of a survey and/or interviews that aim to identify teachers' concerns in the assessment of ELLs. These needs might include:

- how to assess reading and writing skills;

- how to provide scaffolding in the assessment of content area matter; and

- how to prepare students for statewide testing.

Once teachers' needs have been identified, they can be tallied and ranked to help determine priority learning goals. For an example of a professional development needs assessment survey for mainstream teachers, see Figure 6-1. This survey was drafted on the basis of Hall, George, and Rutherford's Stages of Concern (1979) in the implementation of educational innovations. Hall and his colleagues proposed that teachers move through seven stages in using innovations, from lacking awareness of the need for the innovation to being willing to work with others to improve their use of the innovation. The needs identified most frequently by teachers can be used to set the purpose and program goals for the professional development sessions and to identify the resources needed.

Step 3: Start with Standards

Teachers should specify the discipline-specific standards or instructional objectives to be evaluated with the assessments. It is important to identify standards for factual knowledge that can be easily measured with multiple-choice and sentence completion tests and those that can be more appropriately assessed with performance-based assessments. Teachers may want to begin with state and/or local standards in English language arts, science, social studies, or mathematics. For example, teachers in one school district decided to help prepare both elementary and secondary ELLs for the statewide writing assessment in English language arts by preparing a handbook for the teaching and assessment of writing in Grades 1 through 12. Teachers in another school system chose to focus on assessment of reading and writing in elementary level social studies because of the difficulty level of those texts and learning objectives for ELLs.

Step 4: Get Information

Teachers will need to obtain information on the why's and how-to's of using performance-based assessments with English language learners. They can ask a local university or other educational consultant, a knowledgeable administrator, or a teacher experienced in using performance-based assessments to lead workshop sessions that provide teachers with the information

Figure 6-1

Needs Assessment of English Language Learners

Circle the number that is most true of you.

1. Not at all true of me
2. Rarely true of me
3. Sometimes true of me
4. Often true of me
5. Very true of me

Part 1: Second Language Learning

1. I don't see why English language learners can't learn English BEFORE coming into my class.   1 2 3 4 5

2. I want to know if decisions will be made about me based on my effectiveness in helping ESL/bilingual students learn.   1 2 3 4 5

3. I would like to receive information on how bilingual students learn best in English.   1 2 3 4 5

4. I have difficulty finding time to use second language teaching methods.   1 2 3 4 5

5. I want to be a more effective teacher for English language learners.   1 2 3 4 5

6. I want to help other teachers learn about the second language acquisition process and effective teaching methods for English language learners.   1 2 3 4 5

7. I have tried using second language teaching approaches and would like to improve them.   1 2 3 4 5

Part 2: Assessment

8. I don't see why I should learn how to use assessment approaches specific to English language learners.   1 2 3 4 5

9. I want to know if decisions will be made about me based on how well I monitor the progress of English language learners.

10. I would like to receive information on how to use assessment to evaluate the progress of English language learners.   1 2 3 4 5

11. I have problems finding the time to use assessment approaches specific to English language learners.   1 2 3 4 5

12. I want to be able to use assessment to increase the achievement of English language learners.   1 2 3 4 5

13. I would like to help other teachers learn about how to use assessment with English language learners.   1 2 3 4 5

14. I am currently using authentic and performance-based approaches with English language learners and would like to know how to improve them.   1 2 3 4 5

Part 3: Please write short responses to the following questions.

1. What is the one thing you are most concerned about with regard to the assessment of English language learning students?

2. What do you feel are the most important positive aspects of authentic and performance-based assessment for English language learners?

3. What are some specific areas on the assessment of English language learners that you would like to see addressed in future workshops?

4. Other comments?

they need for developing assessment tools for ELLs. Workshops should focus on developing the following competencies:

(1) Understanding the second language acquisition process.

(2) Becoming skilled in the use of effective second language teaching approaches.

(3) Being able to develop and use performance-based assessment tasks and tools for teachers and students to use.

(4) Using assessment results to redirect instruction in order to enhance student learning.

(5) Providing scaffolding in instruction and assessment.

Step 5: Collect Sample Assessment Tools

To save time, assessment study teams should avoid starting from scratch and begin to collect sample assessment tools that fit their purpose. These tools can be collected at conferences, from teacher resource books, from other teachers, and on the Internet. While most of these assessment tools will probably not have been developed for use with ELLs, they can provide ideas for format, language, and content design.

Step 6: Add Scaffolding to Assessments

Once sample assessment tools have been identified, the study team can add to them several types of scaffolding in order to make the language accessible to ELLs. Scaffolding can be added to the language of the items, the format, student response options, and scoring rubrics and self-assessment tools to be used by the students.

Step 7: Try out the Assessments

To determine the usefulness of each assessment tool or task, each teacher on the study team should use the assessments with his or her own English language learners, scoring the products or performances (or reviewing the self-assessment tools), and revising them based on student performance and feedback. Teachers will need to allow time for familiarizing English language learners with the assessment tasks and criteria for assessment. These students should experience success and confidence in using the assessment materials, which may take several trials. Mainstream teachers should also try out the assessment tasks and tools with native speakers of English to see how they perform. If the native speakers perform poorly, the activities and materials should be revised for ELL students, who would probably not do as well as native speakers of English. Members of the study team should then discuss the results of their trials. Will additional scaffolding be needed? Were some criteria left out of the description for excellent performance? Did a student's work exhibit aspects of strength or weakness in a category that had not been considered in the scoring rubric?

Trying out the assessment materials allows for revising the language of the directions and of the assessment tools themselves, clarifying the language of scoring tools so that raters agree on each student's performance, and adjusting the cut scores up or down based on student performance and the availability of other indicators of student proficiency. In addition, feedback obtained from students and teachers during the field-test process can be used to revise the instructional activities and assessment tools. In the development of teacher-made assessments, revision is an ongoing process, one that aims to improve the usefulness, validity, and reliability of each assessment tool. By trying out the rubrics and getting feedback from colleagues, teachers can learn how to revise and improve these scoring tools.

Step 8: Establish Inter-Rater Reliability

If the assessment is for high-stakes purposes, such as placing English language learners in or out of a particular program (for example, transitioning ELLs out of ESOL programs and into the mainstream classroom), the study team will need to establish an acceptable level of inter-rater agreement using the scoring tools. Team members can do this by scoring a number of papers, performances, or other products individually and comparing scores with each other. Rater agreement levels should reach at least 80 percent.

Step 9: Select Anchor Papers or Performances

By scoring student work together and establishing inter-rater reliability, the study team can select those samples of student work that most closely reflect the criteria of the scoring tools at each score point. Using anchor papers and performances can help increase the reliability of any assessment tool by ensuring that raters agree on the language of the scoring tool. Anchor papers can be included in handbooks for each teacher's reference in scoring his or her own students' work, and can also be shared with the students themselves to give them a concrete idea of the requirements for their work.

Step 10: Revise the Assessment Tasks and Tools

Members of the assessment study team should revise the assessment tasks and tools based on discussions and scoring sessions, aiming to improve clarity of the language and fairness of the process. The ultimate purpose of revising the assessment materials is to improve the performance of English language learners.

Additional Strategies

In addition to forming assessment study teams at the building or district level, teachers can find opportunities for professional development on assessment in other collaborative structures such as school-university partnerships, teacher-to-teacher networks within and between schools, and teacher academies (McTighe and Ferrara 1998; National Commission on Teaching and America's Future, 1996; O'Malley and Pierce 1996; Stiggins 1998; Wiggins 1998). Collaborative structures—teacher-designed and directed and organized around problem-solving—allow for inquiry and reflection. These structures can provide several benefits:

- School-university partnerships can promote innovation as part of mutual interests in research and practice.

- Teacher networks can provide a forum for improving content area teaching and for school-wide change.

- Summer teacher academies consisting of school teams and study groups can offer opportunities for intensive learning and shared problem solving.

Making the Commitment of Time

Teachers need professional development opportunities over an extended period of time (not one-shot workshops) in order to help them "digest" and apply the approaches they are learning about. Furthermore, teachers need time to collaborate with other teachers to design and try out new assessments, to discuss what works, and to brainstorm ideas for problem solving. Teachers must be given opportunities to set learning goals and to achieve those goals through an inquiry and data collection process. Unless teachers request and make time for both individual and collaborative study of innovative assessments to be used with ELLs, they will be limited in their ability to use these types of assessment on their own.

Teachers in assessment study teams need to consider making a long-term time commitment to developing and trying out teacher-made assessments to be used with ELLs (Stiggins, 1998; Wiggins,1998; National Commission on Teaching and America's Future, 1996). While Stiggins (1998) has suggested that teachers need 35 to 40 hours each year to read and learn about assessment, try out new assessment approaches in their own classrooms, and meet to share and collaborate with other teachers, even more time may be needed by teachers of ELLs.

Up to 50 percent of the time may have to be spent in team discussions to draft and revise assessment tools. Teachers can study about and experiment with new approaches to assessment and prepare to share findings at team meetings about what worked or didn't work in their classroom and to propose solutions to problems and modifications of existing assessment tools. A realistic time frame for study-team meetings alone might range from three to five half-days over a year's time. Communication could be maintained through email to provide continuity of regular contact. Teachers can agree on a tentative work schedule and individual responsibilities at their first meeting of the year.

Conclusion

To be able to use improved classroom-based assessment practices, teachers need to ask for and obtain professional development opportunities that enable them to manage their own learning process in using assessments for improving the achievement of English language learners. Professional development of a long-term, collegial nature is needed that helps teachers try out assessment tasks and tools and get feedback on the process from colleagues. School study teams and assessment focus groups can lead assessment changes in each school system. When teachers like Marge Smith find their voices and become active in their own professional development, assessment practices can begin to improve the learning of English language learners.

The key to effective assessment of English language learners is information. The author hopes that the information provided in this book helps educators gain an understanding of the second language learning process and the steps they can take to determine their English language learners' progress toward meeting both English language and content area goals and instructional objectives. Classroom teachers need to collaborate with ELL professionals wherever possible in order to provide the most efficient and effective types of instruction and assessment available for English language learners.

APPENDICES

RESOURCE MATERIALS

This section includes three appendices with resources on the instruction and assessment of English language learners.

Appendix A, World Wide Web Sites lists sites for professional organizations and educational clearinghouses and regional laboratories. These web sites provide information either on assessment or on English language learners. Most provide access to databases and online publications.

Appendix B, Professional Organizations provides contact information for three professional organizations that offer publications and conferences on assessment and English language learners. Interested teachers can become members, attend conferences, and/or purchase publications.

Appendix C, Suggested Readings offers suggested readings in a number of different categories, ranging from basic issues in the assessment of English language learners to grading and instructional approaches. While not all titles are about English language learners, each has worthwhile information on assessment or instruction that is applicable to English language learning students.

APPENDIX A

World Wide Web Sites

Each of the Web Sites below can serve as a source of information on either assessment or English language learners. By entering both topic categories in a search, readers will be able to find the most titles on the assessment of ELLs.

Professional Organizations

www.ascd.org　　**Association for Supervision and Curriculum Development (ASCD)**
Offers newsletters, journals, and a wide array of publications, conferences, professional development institutes, and online tutorials on curriculum and assessment

www.nabe.org　　**National Association for Bilingual Education (NABE)**
Offers a newsletter, journal, and other publications, conferences, and legislative policy updates

www.tesol.edu　　**Teachers of English to Speakers of Other Languages (TESOL)**
Provides a newsletter, two journals, and many publications, conferences, and summer academies, as well as information on ESL standards, affiliate news, and a career center.

Educational Clearinghouses and Laboratories

www.cal.org/ericcll   **ERIC Clearinghouse on Languages and Linguistics/ Center for Applied Linguistics**
Has a searchable database and publications online on language teaching, learning, and assessment.

www.ericae.net   **ERIC Clearinghouse on Assessment and Evaluation**
Has a searchable online database and publications on assessment, including a journal.

www.ncbe.gwu.edu   **National Clearinghouse for English Language Acquisition (NCELA)**
Has a searchable database on the education of language minority and English learning students in Grades P through12. Weekly electronic newsletter and publications available online.

www.nwrac.org   **Northwest Regional Educational Laboratory (NWREL) Comprehensive Center, Region X.**
Provides information on assessment in ESL and bilingual education, hot topics, including asking the right questions and lists of assessment instruments.

www.relearning.org   **Relearning by Design**
Formerly the Center on Learning, Assessment, and School Structure(CLASS) directed by Grant Wiggins. Develops video, software, and print materials on assessment and curricular change. Offers conferences, consulting, and sample rubrics.

www.relnetwork.org   **Regional Educational Laboratory Network**
Lists 10 regional labs funded by the U.S. Dept. of Education's Office of Educational Research and Improvement (OERI). Each lab has a specialty area including one on assessment and three on language and cultural diversity), with research updates through publications and technical assistance to schools.

APPENDIX B

Professional Organizations

Professional teacher organizations host annual conventions and regional and affiliate meetings across the country. They also produce publications, including journals, newsletters, and books. Becoming a member of one or more of these organizations and attending their annual meetings can promote networking opportunities for meeting other teachers as well as for gathering information on what teachers are doing in their own classrooms to assess English language learners.

ASCD   **Association for Supervision and Curriculum Development**
1703 N. Beauregard St.
Alexandria, VA 22311-1714
(703) 578-9600 or 1-800-933-ASCD
www.ascd.org

NABE   **National Association for Bilingual Education**
1220 L St., N.W., Suite 605
Washington, DC 20005-4018
(202) 898-1829
www.nabe.org

TESOL   **Teachers of English to Speakers of Other Languages**
700 S. Washington St., Suite 200
Alexandria, VA 22314
(703) 836-0774
www.tesol.edu

APPENDIX C

Suggested Readings

Assessment of Language Learners

Bosswood, T., and R.H. Dwyer. 1995. From marking to feedback: Audiotaped responses to student writing. *TESOL Journal* 5 (2): 20-23.

Brown, J.D. ed. 1998. *New ways of classroom assessment.* Alexandria, Virginia: Teachers of English to Speakers of Other Languages (TESOL).

Cohen, A.D. 1994. *Assessing language ability in the classroom.* Boston: Heinle & Heinle.

Hamayan, E.V, and J.S. Damico. 1991. *Limiting bias in the assessment of bilingual students.* Austin, Texas: Pro-Ed.

Hughes, A. 1989. *Testing for language teachers.* Cambridge, England: Cambridge University Press.

McGovern, S. 1997. Three-peat or how to engage students in revising their oral presentations. *TESOL Journal* 6(3): 32-33.

McNamara, M.J., and D. Deane. 1995. Self-assessment activities: Toward autonomy in language learning. *TESOL Journal* 5 (1): 17-21.

Mohan, B. 1995. Collaborative teacher assessment of ESL writers: Conceptual and practical issues. *TESOL Journal* 5 (1): 28-31.

Murphey, T. 1995. Tests: Learning through negotiated interaction. *TESOL Journal,* 4 (2): 12-16.

O'Malley, J.M., and L. Valdez-Pierce. 1996. *Authentic assessment for English language learners: Practical approaches for teachers.* Reading, Massachusetts: Addison-Wesley.

Smollen, L., C. Newman, T. Wathen, and D. Lee. 1995. Developing student self-assessment strategies. *TESOL Journal* 5 (1): 22-27.

Valdes, G., and R.A. Figueroa. 1994. *Bilingualism and testing: A special case of bias.* Norwood, New Jersey: Ablex.

Performance-Based Assessment

Goodrich, H. 1996/97. Understanding rubrics. *Educational Leadership* 54 (4): 14-17.

Herman, J.L., P.R. Aschbacher, and L. Winters. 1992. *A practical guide to alternative assessment.* Alexandria, Virginia: Association for Supervision and Curriculum Development.

Mitchell, R. 1992. *Testing for learning: How new approaches to evaluation can improve American schools.* New York: Free Press/Macmillan.

Popham, W.J. 1997. What's wrong—and what's right—with rubrics. *Educational Leadership* 55 (2): 72-75.

Wiggins, G. 1998. *Educative assessment.* San Francisco: Jossey-Bass.

Assessment of Reading/Writing

Duke, C.R., and R. Sanchez. 1994. Giving students control over writing assessment. *English Journal* 83 (4): 47-53.

Ferris, D. 1995. Teaching students to self-edit. *TESOL Journal* 4 (4): 18-22.

Gardner, D. 1996. Self-assessment for self-access learners. *TESOL Journal* 5 (3): 18-23.

International Reading Association. 1995. *Reading assessment in practice: Book of readings.* Newark, Delaware: Author.

Jongsma, E., and R. Farr, eds. 1993. *Literacy assessment.* Newark, Delaware: International Reading Association.

Mohan, B., and M. Low. 1995. Collaborative teacher assessment of ESL writers: Conceptual and practical issues. *TESOL Journal* 5 (1): 28-31.

Peregoy, S.F., and O.F. Boyle. 2001. *Reading, writing, and learning in ESL,* 3rd ed. New York: Longman.

Rhodes, L.K. 1993. Literacy assessment: *A handbook of instruments.* Portsmouth, New Hampshire: Heinemann.

Spangenberg-Urbschat, K., and R. Pritchard, eds. 1994. *Kids come in all languages: Reading instruction for ESL students.* Newark, Delaware: International Reading Association.

Tierney, R.J. 1998. Literacy assessment reform: Shifting beliefs, principled possibilities, and emerging practices. *The Reading Teacher* 51 (5): 374-390.

Valencia, S.W., E.H. Hiebert, and P. P. Afflerbach, eds. 1994. *Authentic reading assessment: Practices and possibilities*. Newark, Delaware: International Reading Association.

Portfolio Assessment

Clemmons, J., L. Laase, D. Cooper, N. Areglado, and M. Dill. 1993. *Portfolios in the classroom: A teacher's sourcebook*. Jefferson City, Missouri: Scholastic Professional Books.

Gottlieb, M. 1995. Nurturing student learning through portfolios. *TESOL Journal* 5 (1): 12-14.

Herman, J.L., and L. Winters. 1994. Portfolio research: A slim collection. *Educational Leadership* 52 (2): 48-55.

Khatani, S.A. 1999. FORUM—Electronic portfolios in ESL writing: An alternative approach. *Computer Assisted Language Learning* 12 (3): 261-268.

Grading

Guskey, T.R. 1994. Making the grade: What benefits students? *Educational Leadership* 52 (2): 14-20.

Kohn, A. 1994. Grading: The issue is not how but why. *Educational Leadership* 52 (2): 38-41.

Seeley, M.M. 1994. The mismatch between assessment and grading. *Educational Leadership* 52 (2): 4-6.

Instructional Approaches

Chamot, A.U., and J.M. O'Malley. 1994. *The CALLA Handbook: Implementing the Cognitive Academic Language Learning Approach*. White Plains, New York: Addison-Wesley Longman.

Christison, M.A. 1996. Teaching and learning languages through multiple intelligences. *TESOL Journal* 6 (1): 10-14.

Holt, D.D., B. Chips, and D. Wallace. 1992. *Cooperative learning in the secondary school: Maximizing language acquisition, academic achievement, and social development.* Washington, D.C.: National Clearinghouse for Bilingual Education.

Huerta-Macias, A., and M.L. Gonzalez. 1997. Beyond ESL instruction: Creating structures that promote achievement for all secondary students. *TESOL Journal* 6 (4): 16-19.

Kagan, S. 1994. *Cooperative Learning.* San Clemente, California: Resources for Teachers.

Kessler, C., ed. 1992. *Cooperative language learning:* A teacher's resource book. Englewood Cliffs, New Jersey: Prentice Hall Regents.

Scarcella, R. 1990. *Teaching language minority students in the multicultural classroom.* Englewood Cliffs, New Jersey: Prentice-Hall.

Sperling, D. 1999. *The ESL Internet activity book for students.* Upper Saddle River, New Jersey: Prentice Hall Regents.

Sperling, D. 1998. *Dave Sperling's Internet Guide,* 2nd ed. Upper Saddle River, New Jersey: Prentice Hall Regents.

REFERENCES

August, D., and K. Hakuta, eds. 1998. *Educating language-minority children.* Washington, D.C.: National Academy Press.

Baker, E.L. 1993. Questioning the technical quality of performance assessment. *The School Administrator* 50 (11): 12-16.

Baker, E.L., R.L. Linn, and J.L. Herman. 2002. From the Directors. [Special Issue: "No child left behind."] *The CRESST Line Newsletter* Spring, 1-3.

Bertrand, J.E. 1994. Student assessment and evaluation. In *Assessment and evaluation for student centered learning,* edited by B. Harp. Norwood, Massachusetts: Christopher-Gordon Publishers.

Boser, U. 2001. Pressure without support. [Special issue: Quality Counts 2001. A better balance: Standards, tests, and the tools to succeed]. *Education Week* 20 (17).

Brualdi, A.C. 2002. Traditional and modern concepts of validity. In *What teachers need to know about assessment,* edited by L.M. Rudner and W.D. Schafer. Washington, D.C.: National Education Association.

Calkins, L., K. Montgomery, and D. Santman. 1998. *A teacher's guide to standardized reading tests: Knowledge is power.* Portsmouth, New Hampshire: Heinemann.

Clemmons, J., L. Laase, D. Cooper, N. Areglado, and M. Dill. 1993. *Portfolios in the classroom: A teacher's sourcebook.* Jefferson City, Missouri: Scholastic Professional Books.

Collier, V.P. 1992. A synthesis of studies examining long-term language minority student data on academic achievement. *Bilingual Research Journal* 16: 1 and 2, pp. 187-212.

Collier, V.P., and W. Thomas. 1998. Assessment and evaluation. In *Bilingual and ESL Classrooms, Teaching in Multicultural Contexts,* 2nd ed. edited by C.J. Ovando and V.P. Collier. Boston: McGraw-Hill.

Cummins, J. 1994a. Primary language instruction and the education of language minority students. In *Schooling and language minority students: A theoretical framework*, 2nd ed., edited by C.F. Leyba. Los Angeles: California State University, Evaluation, Dissemination, and Assessment Center.

Cummins, J. 1994b. The acquisition of English as a second language. In *Kids come in all languages: Reading instruction for ESL students* edited by K. Spangenberg-Urbschat and R. Pritchard. Newark, Delaware: International Reading Association.

Cummins, J. 1989. *Empowering minority students*. Sacramento, California: California Association for Bilingual Education.

Cummins, J. 1984. *Bilingualism and special education: Issues in assessment and pedagogy*. Clevedon, England: Multilingual Matters.

Ellis, R. 1994. *The study of second language acquisition*. Oxford, England: Oxford University Press.

Fielding, L.G., and P.D. Pearson. 1994. Reading comprehension: What works. *Educational Leadership* 51 (5): 62-68.

Fisher, D., D. Lapp, J. Flood, and L. Suarez. 2001. Assessing bilingual students when policies and practices meet in the classroom. In *Literacy assessment of second language learners*, edited by S.R. Hurley and J.V. Tinajero. Boston: Allyn and Bacon.

Feuer, M. J., and K. Fulton. 1993. The many faces of performance assessment. *Phi Delta Kappan* 74 (6): 478.

Fradd, S.H., and O. Lee. 2001. Needed: A framework for integrating standardized and informal assessment for students developing academic language proficiency in English. In *Literacy assessment of second language learners*, edited by S.R. Hurley and J.V. Tinajero. Boston: Allyn and Bacon.

Frisby, C.L. 2001. Academic achievement. In *Handbook of multicultural assessment*, edited by L.A. Suzuki, J.G. Ponterotto, and P.J. Meller, 2nd ed. San Francisco: Jossey-Bass.

Garcia, G.E., and P.D. Pearson. 1994. Assessment and diversity. *Review of Research in Education* 20: 337-391.

Gottlieb, M. 1999. *Standards-based alternate assessments for limited-English-proficient students: A guide for Wisconsin educators.* Prepublication draft. Madison: Wisconsin Department of Public Instruction.

Hall, G.E., A.A. George, and W.L. Rutherford. 1979. *Measuring stages of concern about the innovation: A manual for use of the SoC questionnaire.* Austin: University of Texas.

Hamayan, E.V., and J.S. Damico. 1991. *Limiting bias in the assessment of bilingual students.* Austin: Pro-Ed.

Harp, B. 1994. Principles of assessment and evaluation in whole language classrooms. In *Assessment and evaluation for student-centered learning,* edited by B. Harp, 2nd ed. Norwood, Massachusetts: Christopher-Gordon Publishers.

Herman, J.L., P.R. Aschbacher, and L. Winters. 1992. *A practical guide to alternative assessment.* Alexandria, Virginia: Association for Supervision and Curriculum Development.

Heubert, J.P., and R.M. Hauser, eds. 1999. *High-stakes: Testing for tracking promotion, and graduation.* Washington, D.C.: National Academy Press.

Kindler, A. 2002. Survey of the states' limited English proficient students and available educational programs and services: 1999-2000. Summary report. Washington, D.C.: National Clearinghouse for English Language Acquisition. Retrieved 7/12/02 from http://www.ncbe.gwu.edu/states/index.htm

Kolls, M. 1992. Portfolio assessment: A feasibility study. Paper presented at the March annual meeting of Teachers of English to Speakers of Other Languages, Vancouver, B.C., Canada.

Krashen, S.D. 1994. Bilingual education and second language acquisition theory. In *Schooling and language minority students: A theoretical framework,* 2nd ed., edited by C. F. Leyba. Los Angeles: California State University, Evaluation, Dissemination, and Assessment Center.

Marzano, R.J., and J. S. Kendall. 1998. *Implementing standards-based education.* Washington, D.C.: National Education Association.

Marzano, R.J., D. Pickering, and J. McTighe. 1993. *Assessing student outcomes: Performance assessment using the Dimensions of Learning model.* Alexandria, Virginia: Association for Supervision and Curriculum Development.

McNeil, L.M. 2000. *Contradictions of school reform: Educational costs of standardized testing.* New York: Routledge.

McTighe, J., and S. Ferrara. 1998. *Assessing learning in the classroom.* Washington, D.C.: National Education Association.

Mitchell, R. 1992. *Testing for learning: How new approaches to evaluation can improve American schools.* New York: The Free Press.

National Commission on Teaching & America's Future. 1996. *What matters most: Teaching for America's Future.* New York: Author.

National Foundation for the Improvement of Education. 1996. *Teachers take charge of their learning: Transforming professional development for student success.* Washington, D.C.: Author.

No Child Left Behind Act of 2001, 1 U.S.C.A. and 1001 *et seq.* (National Clearinghouse for Bilingual Education 2001)

No Child Left Behind Act of 2001. 3 U.S.C. A. and 3001 *et. seq.* (National Clearinghouse for Bilingual Education 2001).

"No child left behind" test increases unlikely to be met. 2002. *The CRESST Line Newsletter Editor* Spring, 4-5.

Olson, J.F., I.A. Jones, and L.A. Bond. 2001. *State student assessment programs: Annual survey, Data volume II.* Washington, D.C.: Council of Chief State School Officers.

O'Malley, J.M., and L.V. Pierce. 1996. *Authentic assessment for English language learners: Practical approaches for teachers.* White Plains, New York: Addison-Wesley Longman.

O'Malley, J.M., and L.V. Pierce. 1994. State assessment policies, practices, and language minority students. *Educational Assessment* 2 (3): 213-255.

Paige, R. 2002. Dear colleague letter to education officials regarding implementation of "No Child Left Behind". Washington, D.C.: U.S. Dept. of Education. Retrieved 7/26/02 from http://www.ed.gov/News/Letters/020724.html

Ramirez, J., S. Yuen, D. Ramey, and D. Billings. 1991. *Final report: Longitudinal study of structured English immersion strategy, early-exit and late-exit bilingual education programs for language minority children,* Vols. I and II, No. 300-87-0156. San Mateo, California: Aguirre International.

Rudner, L.M., and W.D. Schafer. 2002. *What teachers need to know about assessment*. Washington, D.C.: National Education Association.

Stiggins, R.J. 2002. Assessment crisis: The absence of assessment *FOR* learning. *Phi Delta Kappan* 83 (10): 758-765.

Stiggins, R.J. 1998. *Classroom assessment for student success*. Washington, D.C.: National Education Association.

Suzuki, L.A., J.G. Ponterotto, and P.J. Meller, eds. 2001. *Handbook of multicultural assessment*, 2nd ed. San Francisco: Jossey-Bass.

Thomas, W.P., and V.P. Collier. 2002. *A national study of school effectiveness for language minority students' long-term academic achievement: Executive Summary*. Washington, D.C.: National Clearinghouse for English Language Acquisition.

U.S. Congress. 2001. Elementary and Secondary Education Act (Reauthorized). Washington, D.C.: Author.

U.S. Department of Education. 2002. Paige outlines adequate yearly progress provisions under No Child Left Behind. Press Release. Washington, D.C.: Author. Retrieved 7/26/02 from http://www.ed.gov/PressReleases/07-2002/07242002.html

Virginia Board of Education. 1995. *Standards of Learning for Virginia Public Schools*. Richmond, Virginia: Author.

Wiggins, G. 1998. *Educative assessment: Designing assessments to inform and improve student performance*. San Francisco: Jossey-Bass.

Wiggins, G. 1989. Teaching to the (authentic) test. *Educational Leadership* 46 (7): 41-47.

Wood, K.D. 2001. *Literacy strategies across the subject areas*. Boston: Allyn and Bacon.